SWISS ART

LOCATIONS

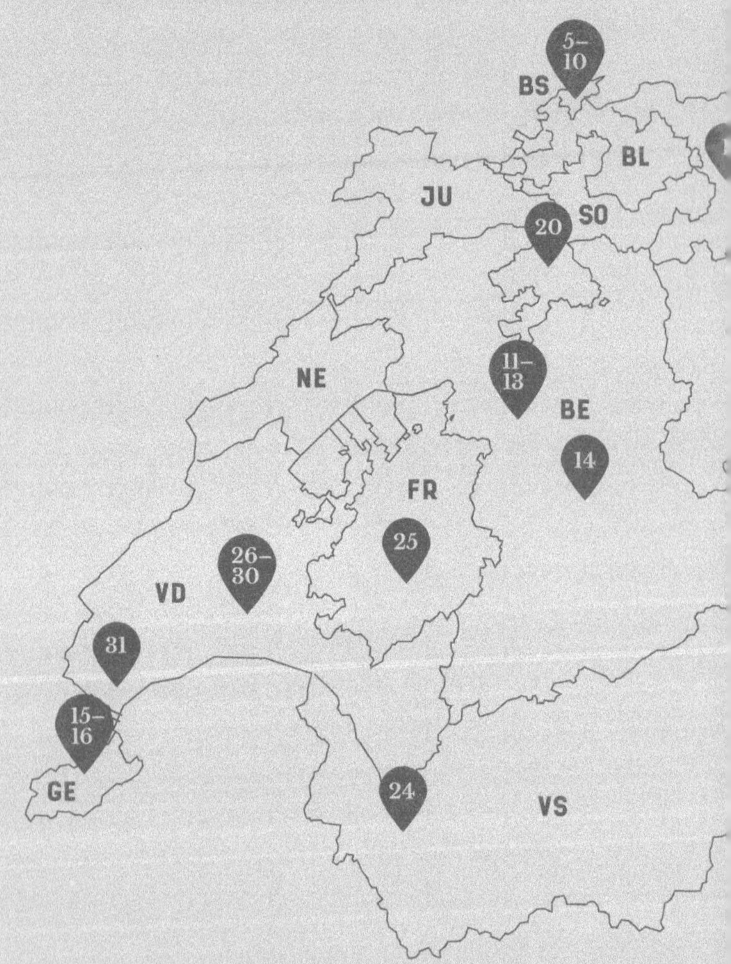

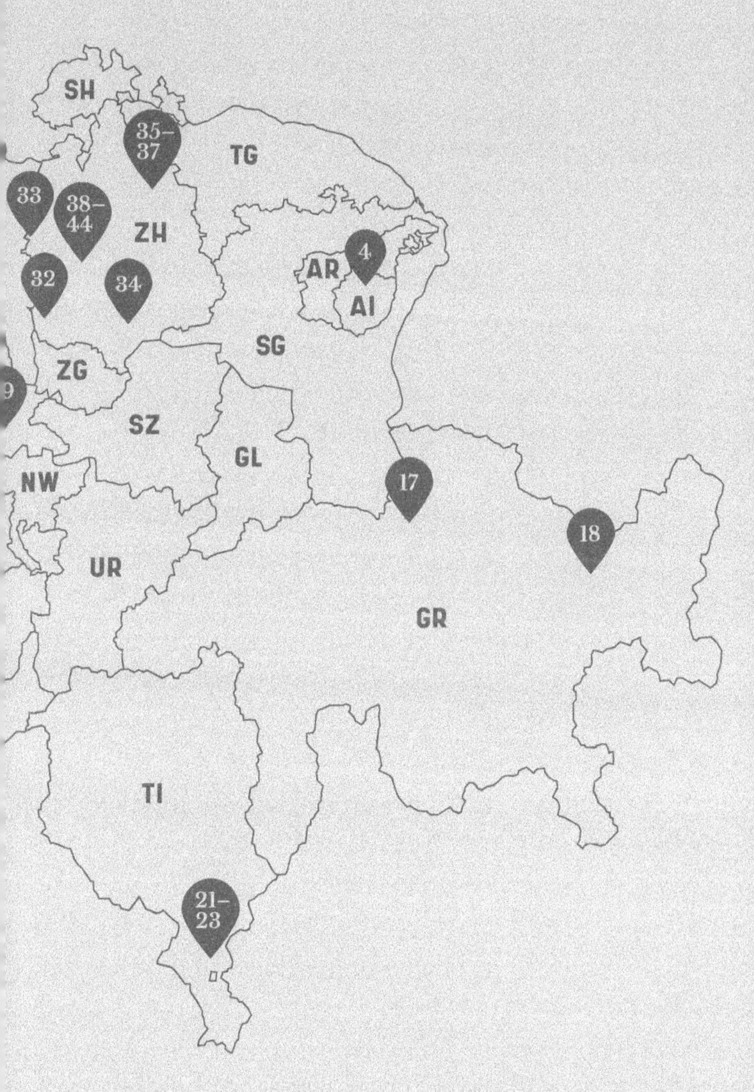
SH
35–
37
TG
33
38–
44
ZH
4
AR
AI
32
34
SG
ZG
SZ
GL
NW
17
18
UR
GR
TI
21–
23

Bergli Books is being supported by the Swiss Federal Office of Culture with a structural grant for the years 2021–2025.

Swiss Art
The unmissable galleries and museums

Author: © Katrin Gygax
Illustrations, typesetting and layout: Chloé Châtelain and Ajša Zdravković
Photography: Image credits pp.156–158
Editor: Angela Wade

ISBN: 978-3-03869-166-2
First edition: September 2024

An imprint of HELVETIQ SA
Mittlere Strasse 4
4056 Basel
Switzerland

Bergli

SWISS ART

The unmissable galleries and museums

Katrin Gygax

B•

TABLE OF

Introduction	6
Aargauer Kunsthaus	8
Museum Langmatt	10
Stapferhaus	14
Kunstmuseum-Kunsthalle Appenzell	18
Kunstmuseum Basel	22
Cartoonmuseum Basel	26
Museum Tinguely	28
Art Basel	32
Von Bartha	34
Fondation Beyeler	38
Zentrum Paul Klee	42
Kunsthalle Bern	44
Swiss art statistics	46
Kunstmuseum Bern	48
Kunstmuseum Thun	50
Musée d'Art et d'Histoire de Genève	54
Ports Francs et Entrepôts de Genève	58
Central Geneva art galleries map	60
Bündner Kunstmuseum Chur	62
Muzeum Susch	66
Sammlung Rosengart	70
Kunstmuseum Solothurn	74
Swiss art patrons	78

Marco Lucchetti Art Gallery 80
Bally Foundation Villa Heleneum 82
MASI Lugano and Collezione Giancarlo e Danna Olgiati 86
Fondation Pierre Gianadda 90
HR Giger Museum 92
Collection de l'Art Brut 98
Plateforme 10: MCBA, mudac and Photo Elysée 100
Fondation de l'Hermitage 104
Château de Prangins 106
Bugs that eat art 110
Schweizerisches Nationalmuseum Sammlungszentrum 112
Bruno Weber Park 114
Galerie Bruno Bischofberger 116
Fotomuseum Winterthur 118
Kunst Museum Winterthur 122
Sammlung Oskar Reinhart "Am Römerholz" 128
Stiftung für Kunst, Kultur und Geschichte (SKKG) 132
Löwenbräukunst-Areal: Haus Konstruktiv, Kunsthalle Zürich and Migros Museum für Gegenwartskunst 136
Kunsthaus Zürich 140
Museum Rietberg 148
Museum für Gestaltung Zürich 152
Image credits 156
About the author 160

CONTENTS

ALL THAT MONEY HAS TO GO

Thanks to its ability to fund large projects, Switzerland has just over 160 non-commercial art galleries and art museums in a country of just under nine million people. These spaces do not limit themselves to exhibitions and tours of world-class art from all around the world; nowadays, they also include public outreach programs, storytelling, classes for kids, art and dine events, and, significantly, provenance research commissions.

It was hard selecting these 44 from the 162 possibilities. A special mention certainly needs to go to the following:

- Schaulager Basel houses the collection of the Emanuel Hoffmann Foundation and is accessible only for tours and special exhibitions.

- Every year, the exomusée in Le Locle commissions more street artists to officially convert the town center into an outdoor museum. It's an impressive exhibition that keeps growing over time.

- The vibrant, family-friendly Maison d'Ailleurs in Yverdon-les-Bains focuses on the world of science fiction and its interplay between popular culture, contemporary art and general science.

Please note: It is the nature of Swiss art museums to close for renovations or move to larger, fancier premises. Please always check the gallery's website (listed at the bottom of each page) before you go.

SOMEWHERE

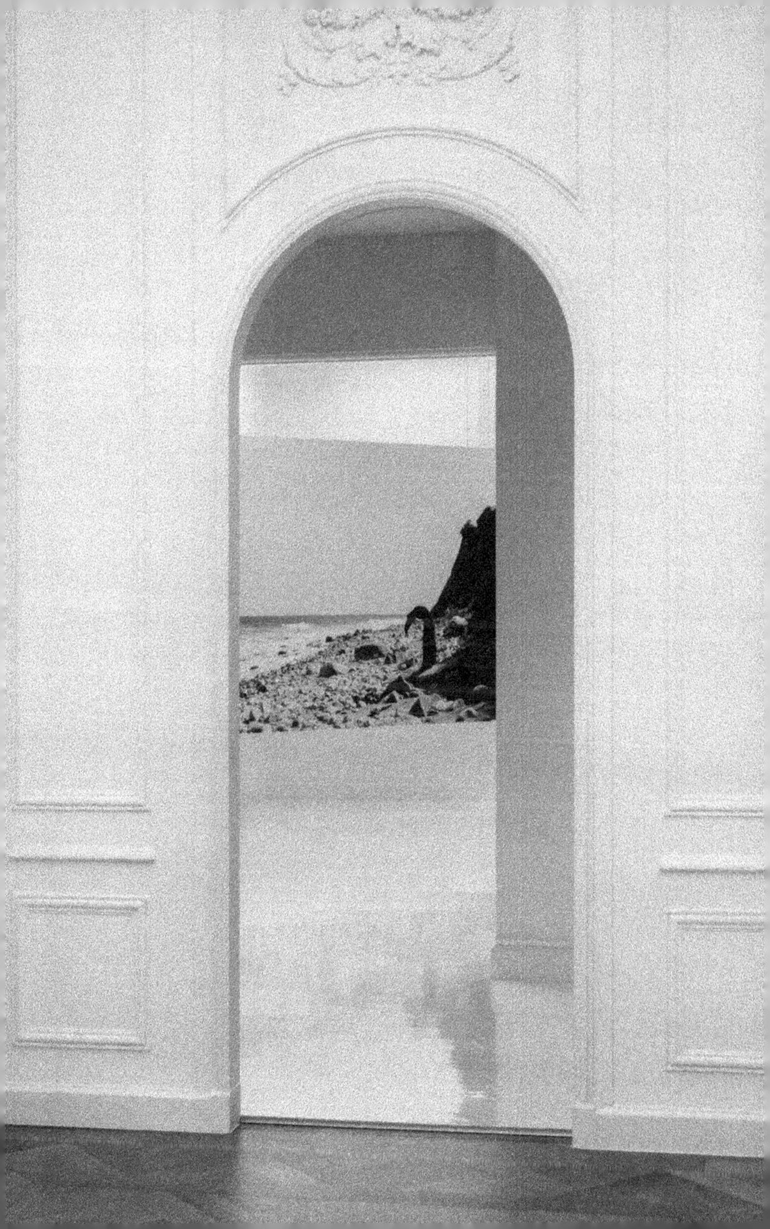

AARGAUER KUNSTHAUS

— *A cosmopolitan vibe at the edge of Aarau's old town*

An addition, designed by architects Herzog & de Meuron, spiffs up this home to a sizeable art collection ranging from the 18th century to the present. Aargauer Kunsthaus focuses on Swiss talent, like Johann Heinrich Füssli, Alice Bailly and Silvia Bächli, and more than meets its aim to bring art appreciation to all and sundry. This is also thanks to its very popular FLOWERS TO ARTS exhibition, an annual spring event that matches impressive real-life arrangements to works in the museum and captures the true admiration of all—from enthusiastic kids to otherwise snooty old art critics. Its Basil café is a local hotspot with a special flair for baked goods, like the cinnamon buns that also tempt visitors with a Nutella option.

AARGAUERPLATZ, 5001 AARAU
AARGAUERKUNSTHAUS.CH

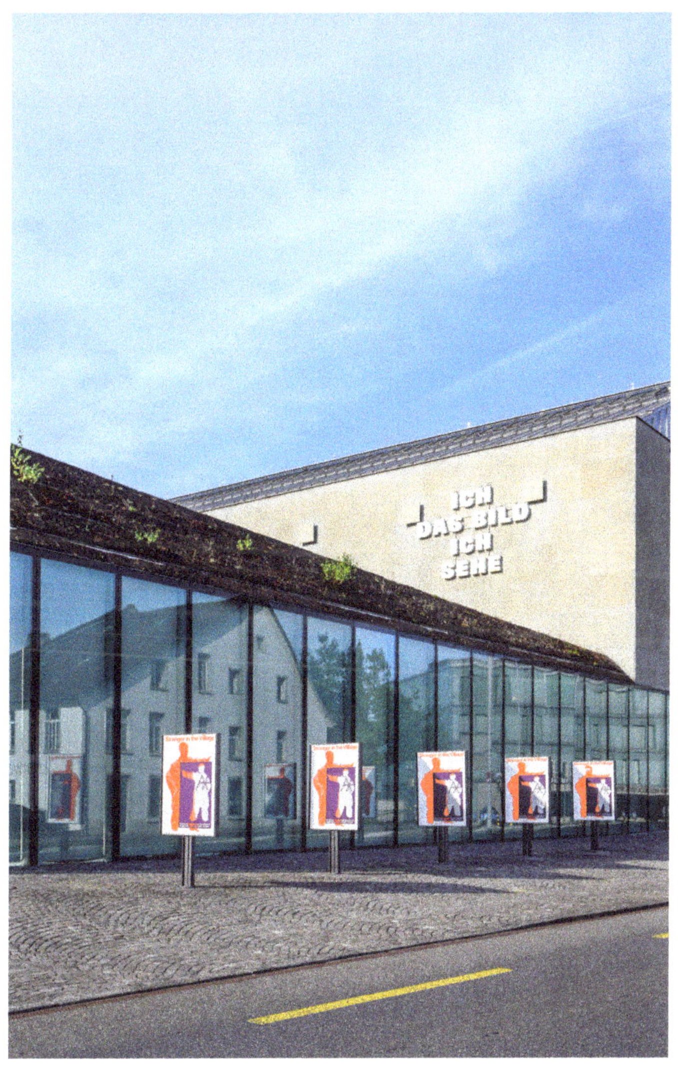
ICH
DAS BILD
ICH
SEHE
Stranger in the Village

MUSEUM LANGMATT

— *A private collection in historical surroundings*

This small museum gained international attention in 2023 for auctioning off three Cezannes to save itself from closure. Built between 1899 and 1901 by industrialist collectors Sidney and Jenny Brown-Sulzer, the Villa Langmatt became their private gallery. Many of the invited guests did not appreciate pieces by "insane" French painters like Degas, Gauguin, Monet and Renoir. Undeterred, the Brown-Sulzers continued to collect their works. With much of the collection now displayed more or less as it would have been 100 years ago, the Langmatt is often a fascinating time capsule. Today, contemporary artists, such as Ash Keating and Natacha Donzé, are regularly given the opportunity to add their own style to the rooms or develop works for the lush gardens as part of juxtaposing exhibitions. Do not miss the simple but gorgeous veranda café for coffee and cake.

RÖMERSTRASSE 30, 5401 BADEN
LANGMATT.CH

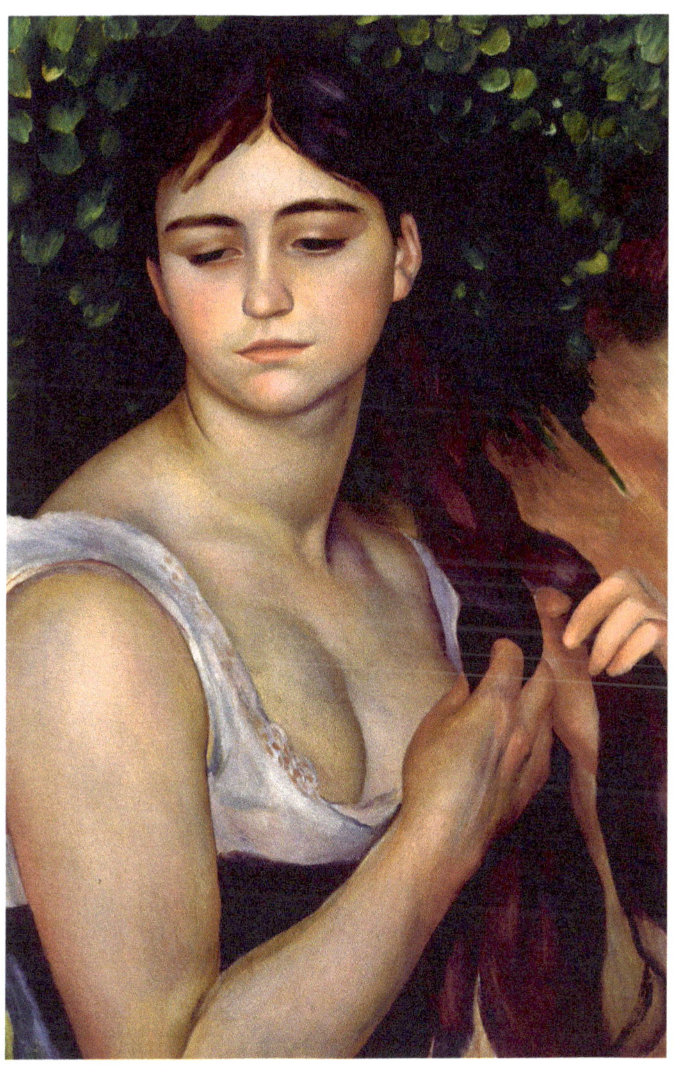

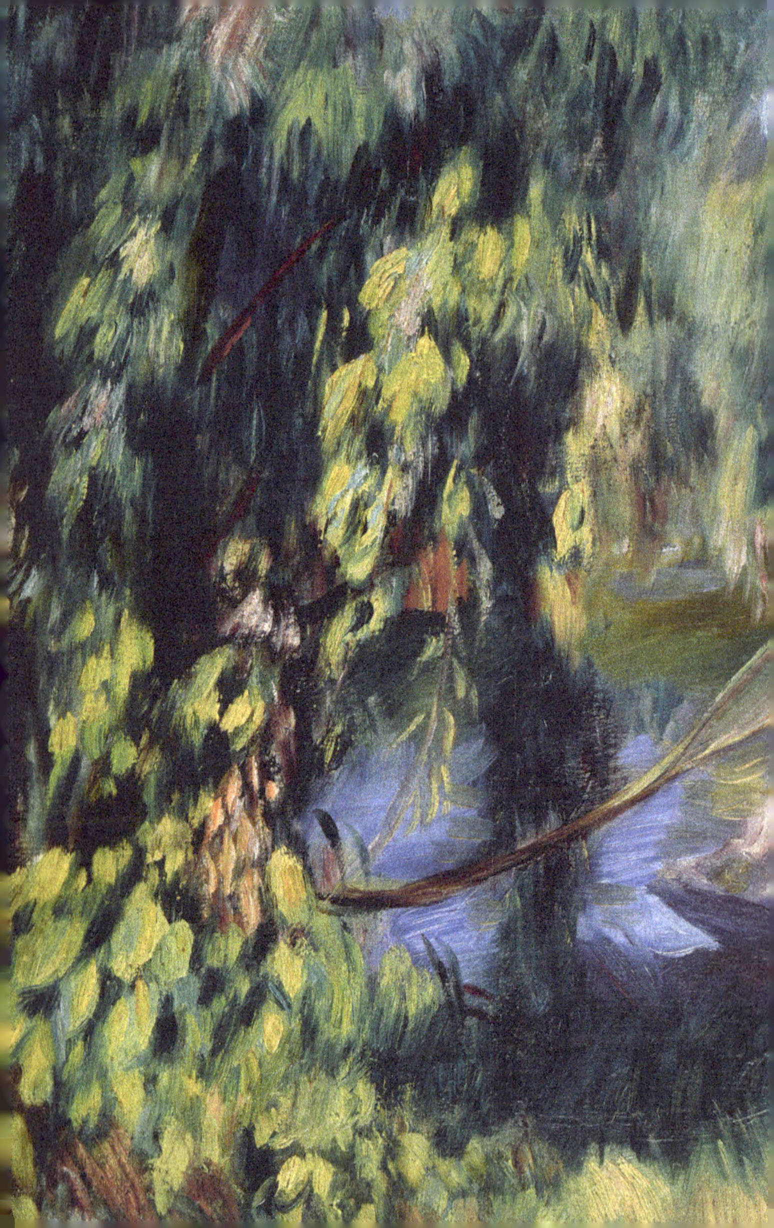

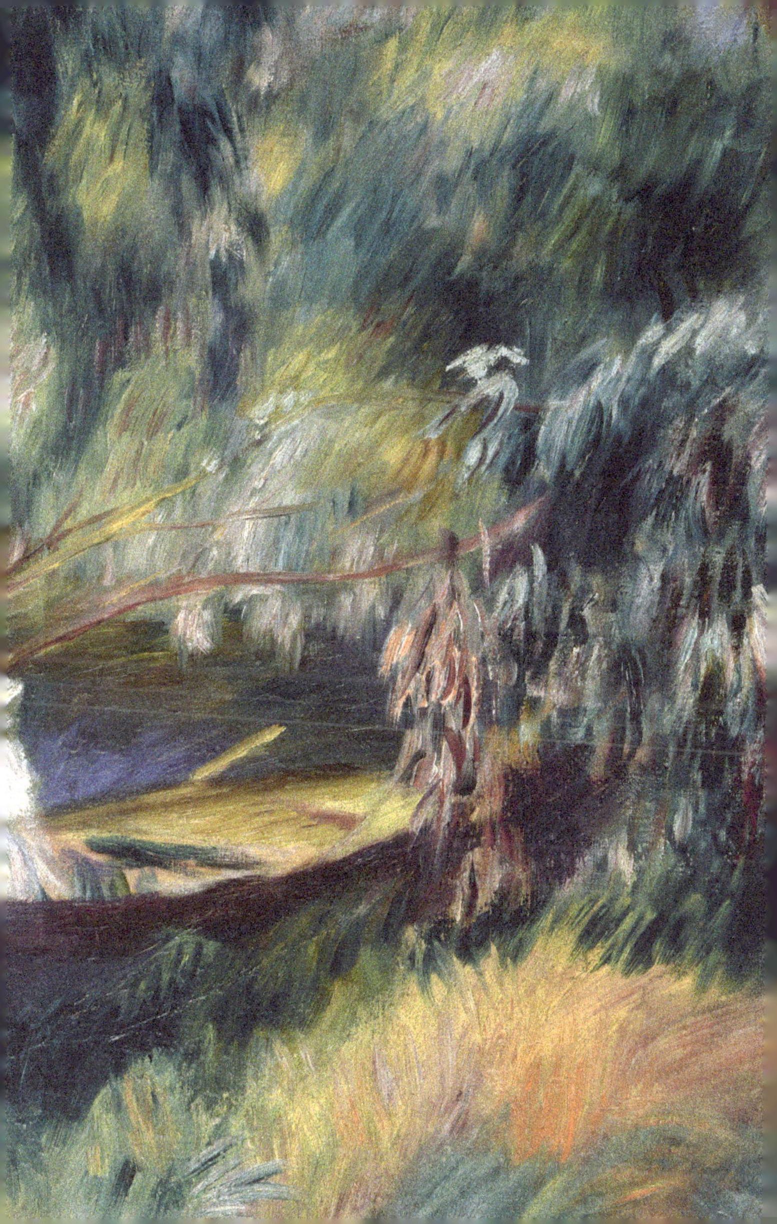

STAPFERHAUS

— *Where arts-based dialog takes on today's society*

This purpose-built, flexible exhibition space takes on issues of the day—like fake news, money, gender, the environment—adding art, design and everyday objects to underline the topic and inspire visitors to join in the discussion. With the outside of the building included in the exhibition design, the experience already begins from across the street as you emerge from the train station or parking lot. Exhibitions are generally a collaboration between designers, historians, psychologists, researchers—and sometimes even car manufacturers. Aimed at all walks of life and ages, accessibility and inclusion are at the forefront: mobility, hearing and visual impairments are taken into consideration. This is a kid-friendly museum as well, thanks to dedicated, hands-on installations and activities. Don't leave without trying the raspberry tarts in the Stapferhaus Bistro.

BAHNHOFSTRASSE 49, 5600 LENZBURG
STAPFERHAUS.CH

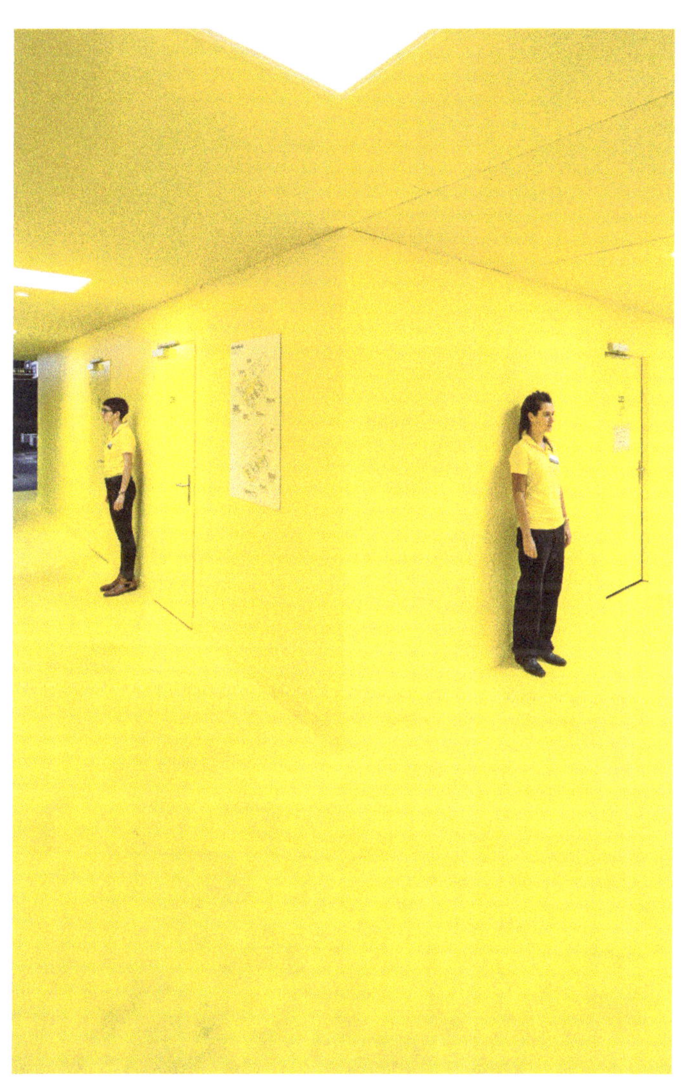

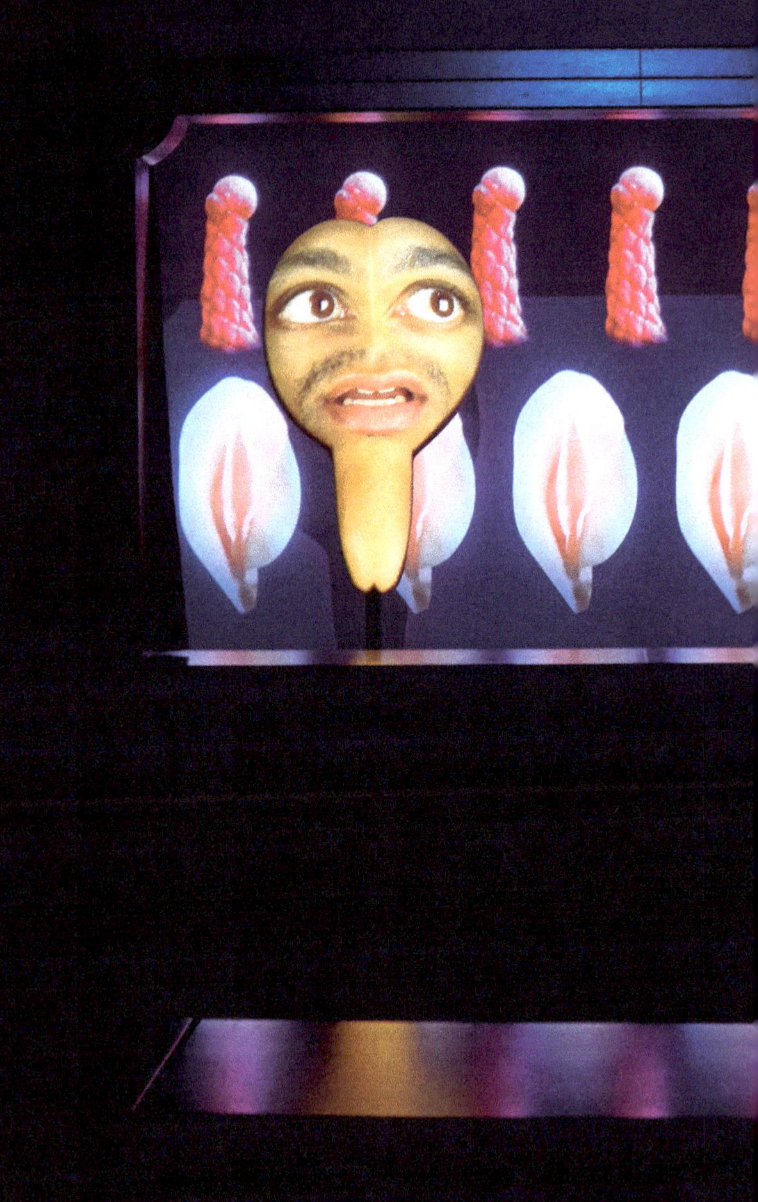

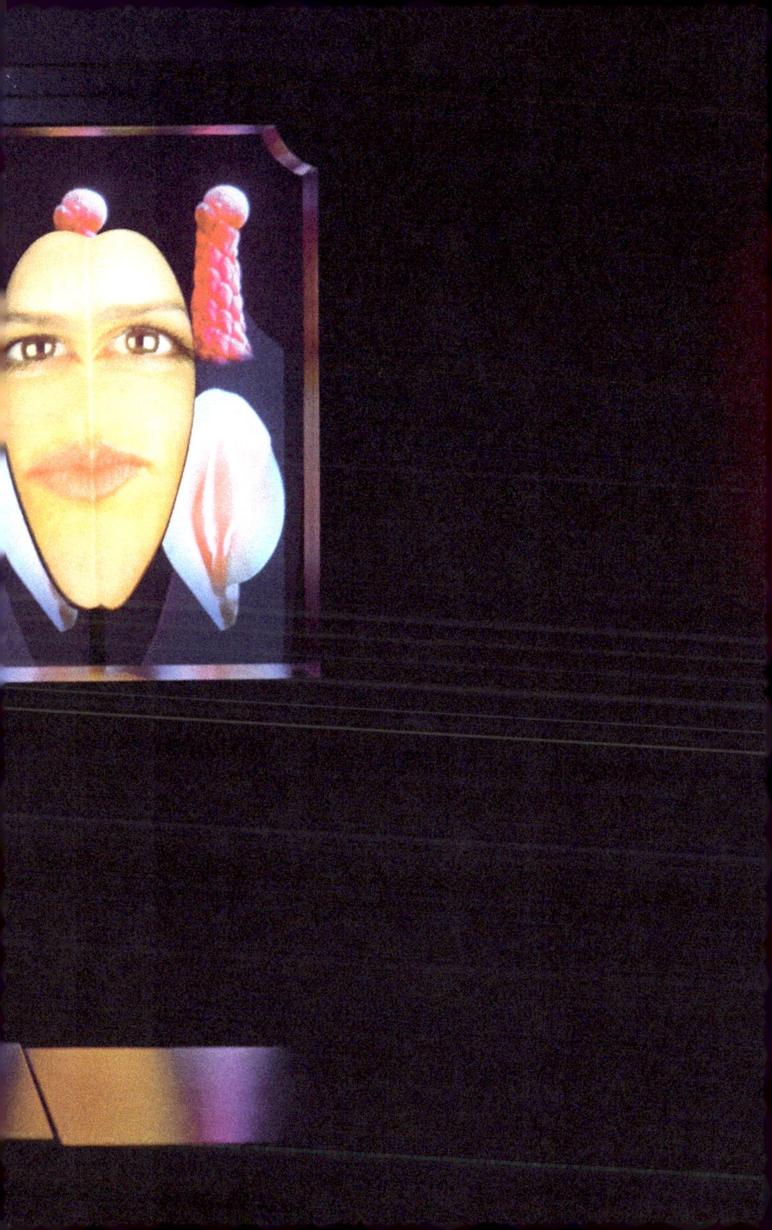

KUNSTMUSEUM-KUNSTHALLE APPENZELL

— *Modern art spaces at the center of Swiss folk tradition*

If you are part of a group that can never decide on a cultural destination, go to Appenzell. Fans of cows, bells and cheese will be pleased, as will those who love discovering modern and contemporary art. Just behind the train station, the Kunstmuseum—an airy space for world-class thematic and monographic exhibitions—makes the most of the luxuriant green countryside by framing it in windows, like living snapshots. It's home to a collection and shows by today's contemporary artists like the American Liz Craft. Further up the hill, the Kunsthalle hosts conceptual exhibitions that are often developed in close collaboration with artists and allow for experimentation. The former tile factory also holds concerts—everything from flamenco artists to classical pianists. Its old oven is a work of art in itself and a great place for kids to explore. Upstairs houses a library and a small café.

UNTERRAINSTRASSE 5 /
ZIEGELSTRASSE 14, 9050 APPENZELL
KUNSTMUSEUM-KUNSTHALLE.CH

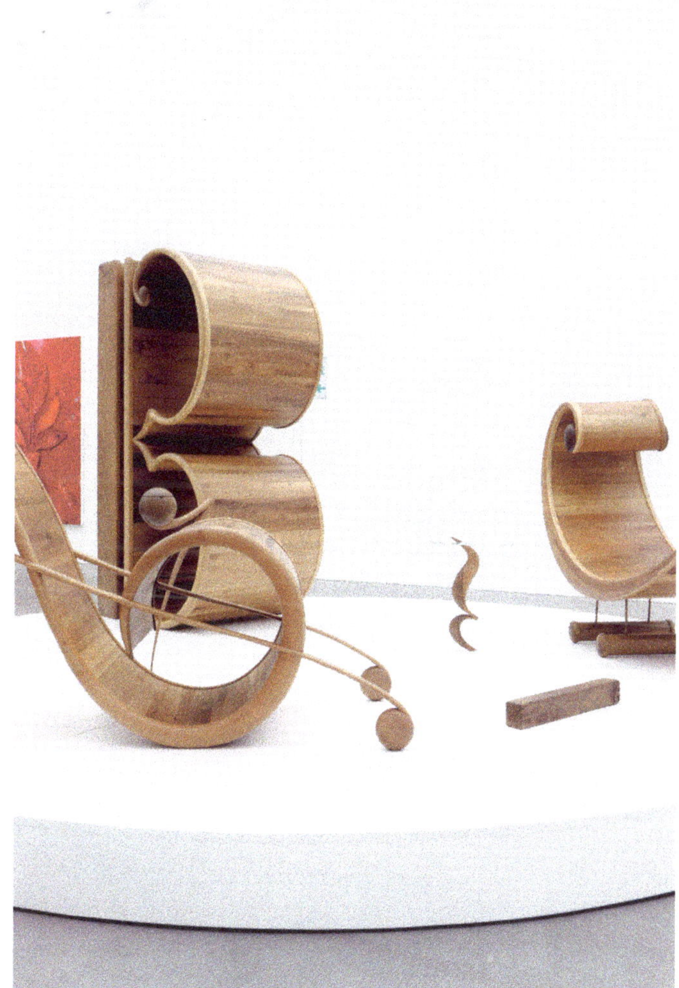

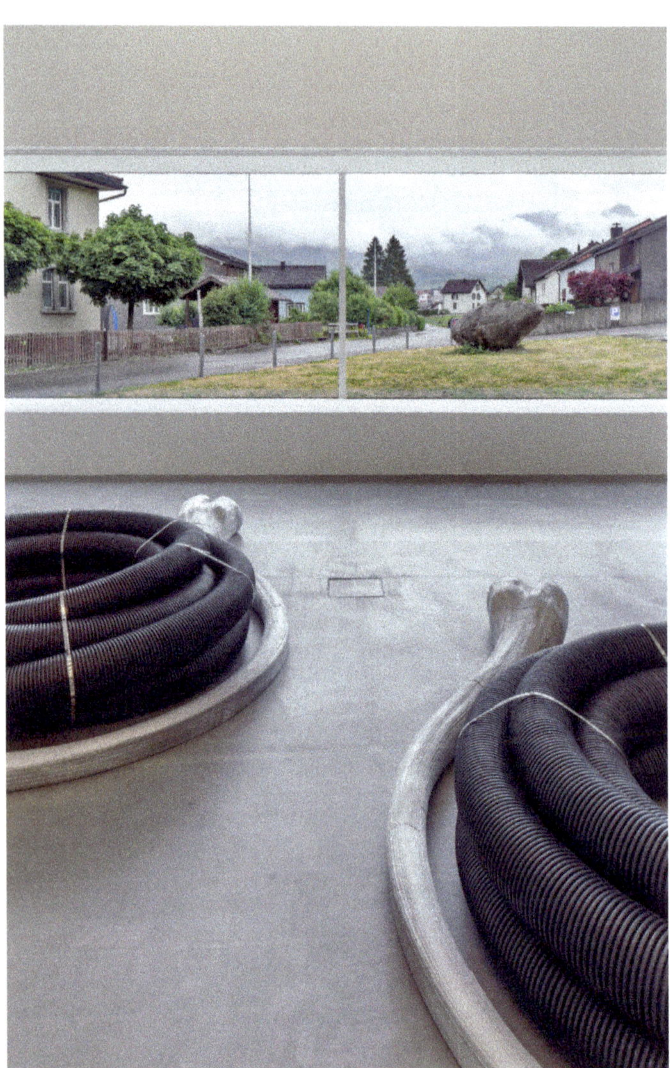

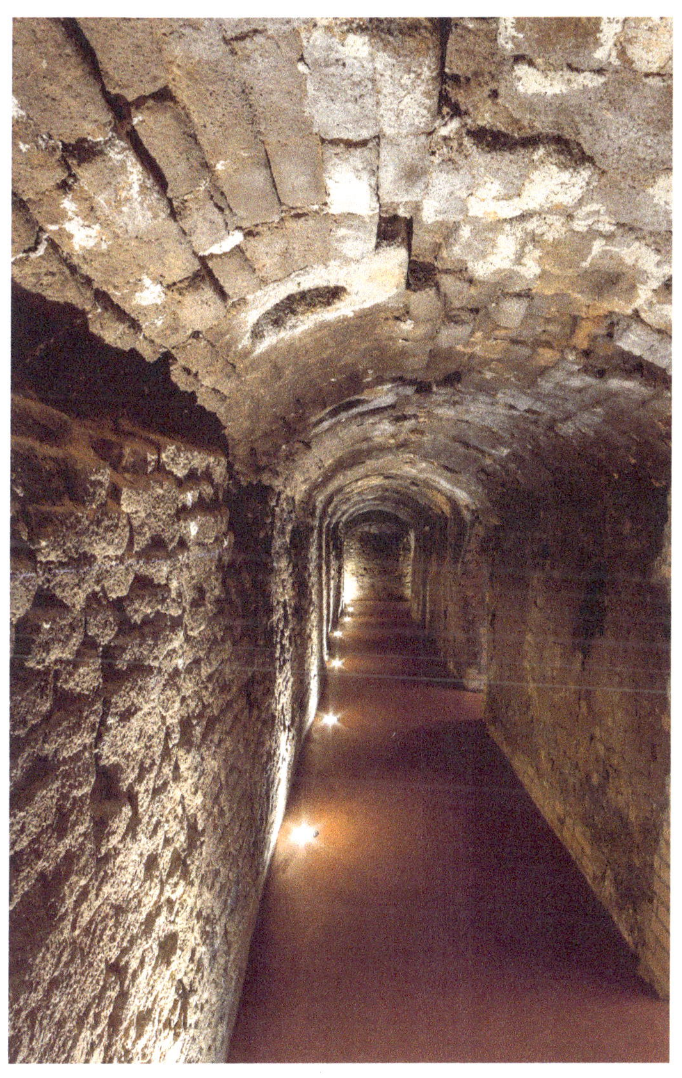

KUNSTMUSEUM BASEL

— *The oldest public collection in the world*

Starting with a private collection acquired by the city and made public in 1671, the Kunstmuseum Basel's artworks have grown to include over 300,000 pieces. Covering international movements from the 14th century to the present, they now include significant works by Lucas Cranach the Elder, Ernst Ludwig Kirchner and Louise Lawler. In recent years, there has finally been a focus on women who were pretty much ignored in the past, such as Paula Modersohn-Becker, Augusta Roszmann and Louise Breslau. An underground tunnel connects the main-collection building, built in 1936, to a modern monolith, conceived for special exhibitions, across the street. A separate museum, a ten-minute walk away on the Rhine, is dedicated to contemporary art. The bistro spills out into the main building's courtyard on warm days; the fun menu bounces around the world, but you're here for the homemade cakes and tortes.

KUNSTMUSEUM BASEL
ST. ALBAN-GRABEN 8, 4010 BASEL

KUNSTMUSEUM BASEL – GEGENWART
ST. ALBAN-RHEINWEG 60, 4052 BASEL
KUNSTMUSEUMBASEL.CH

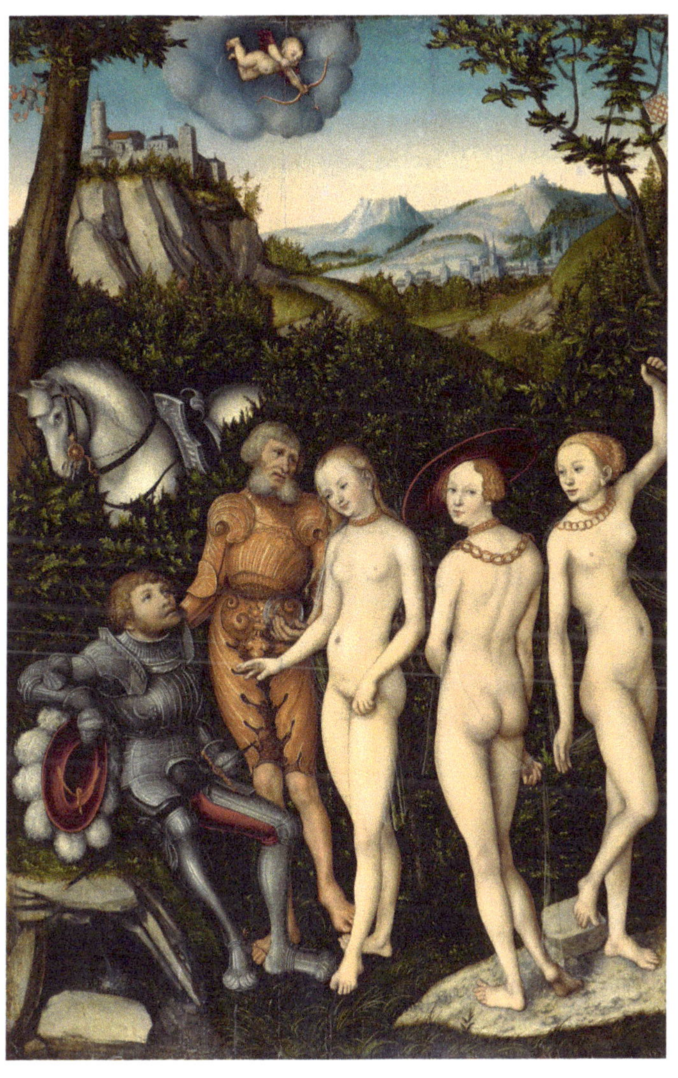

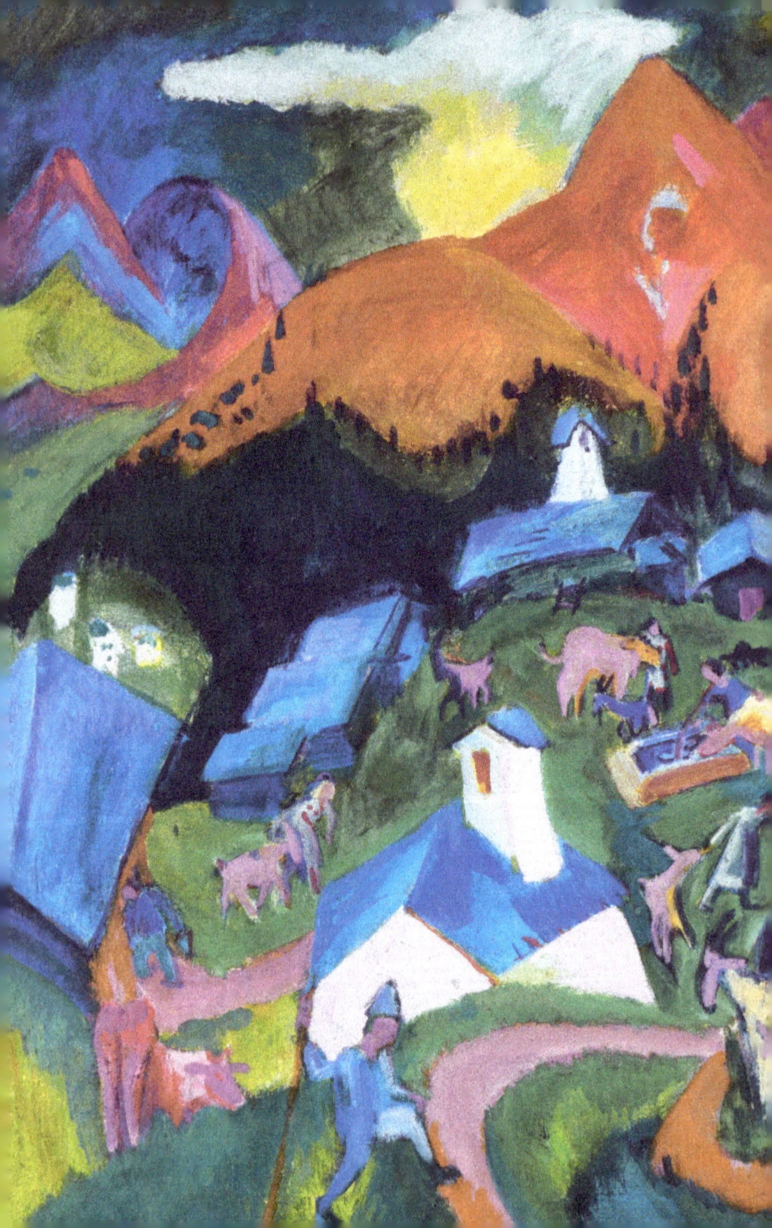

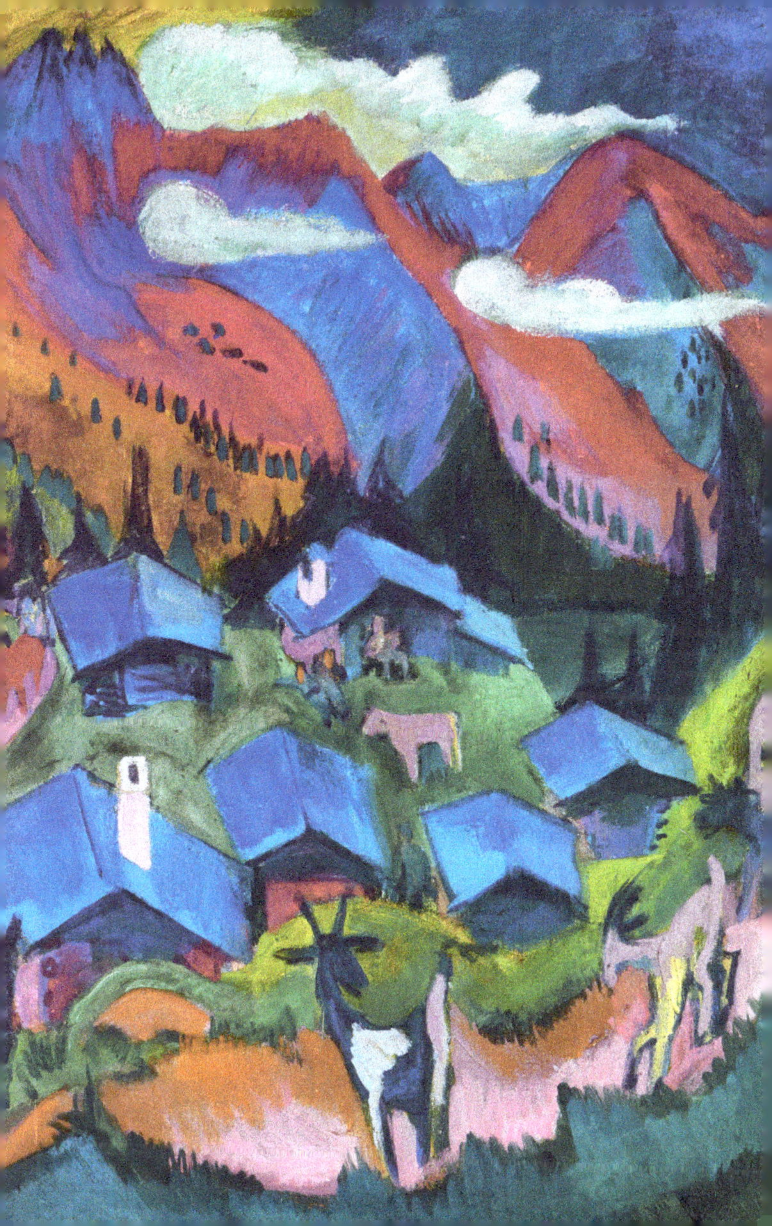

CARTOONMUSEUM BASEL

— *A tiny townhouse stuffed with drawn stories*

Based on the caricature and cartoon collection of local patron Dieter Burckhardt, Cartoonmuseum Basel today encompasses over 10,000 original pieces of narrative by Swiss and international artists. Exhibitions aimed at international audiences are themed or focused on artists, like Dominique Goblet and Richard McGuire, and spread over three floors of a tiny Medieval townhouse enhanced by a modern addition. Lounge in the well-stocked, in-house library and browse through a collection of Finnish comics or *Heckling Hitler: Caricatures of the Third Reich*. The bookshop has a small selection of English comics. The museum is too small for its own café, but there are plenty of options in the surrounding area. Only the ground floor is accessible for wheelchairs.

ST. ALBAN-VORSTADT 28, 4052 BASEL
CARTOONMUSEUM.CH

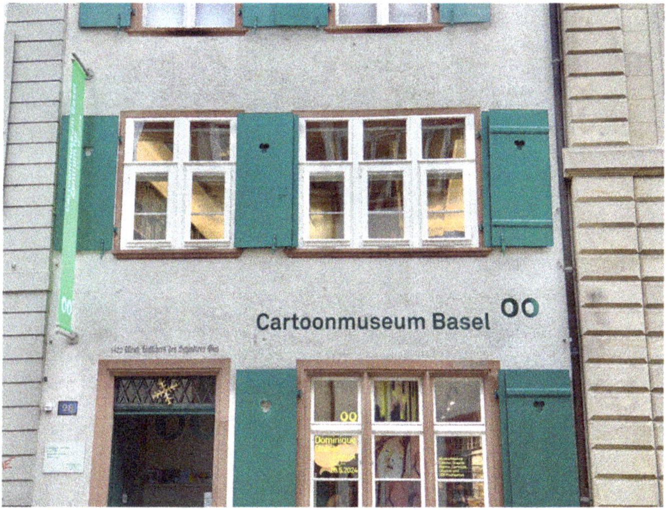
Cartoonmuseum Basel

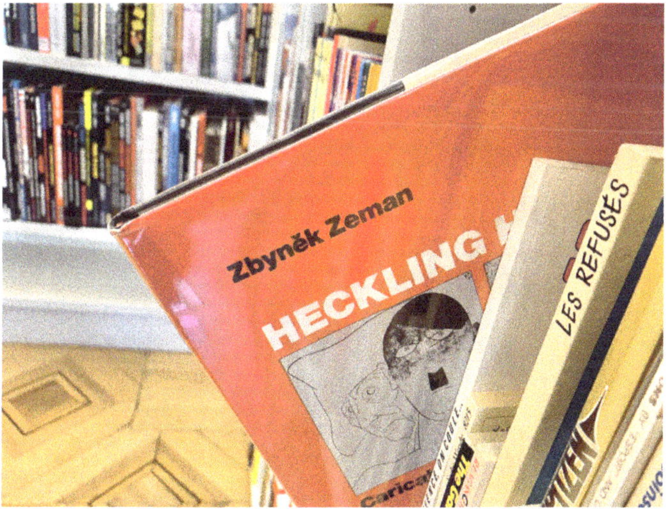
Zbyněk Zeman
HECKLING
LES REFUSÉS

MUSEUM TINGUELY

— *Celebrating a great Swiss artist*

There's always a reason to visit the largest Jean Tinguely collection in the world. Housed in a major work by Swiss architect Mario Botta, the museum lounges in a park by the Rhine River in the middle of Basel. While stuffed with Tinguely's paintings and sculptures, it also curates exhibitions (over 120 so far) of his contemporaries, including Niki de Saint Phalle and Yves Klein, as well as socially conscious artists of today, like Otto Piene and Mika Rottenberg. Botta's large spaces do Tinguely's machine sculptures justice, while a fascinating glassed-in workshop lets you watch experts restore pieces that need more than just a little oil or a tightened screw. Its daytime bistro, Chez Jeannot, has a French-Med flavor and the wines to go with it. The grounds extend to the riverbank; bring your swimsuit in summer and float down to Dreirosen Bridge, your last chance to get out before the international river port, where swimming is prohibited.

PAUL SACHER-ANLAGE 1, 4058 BASEL
TINGUELY.CH

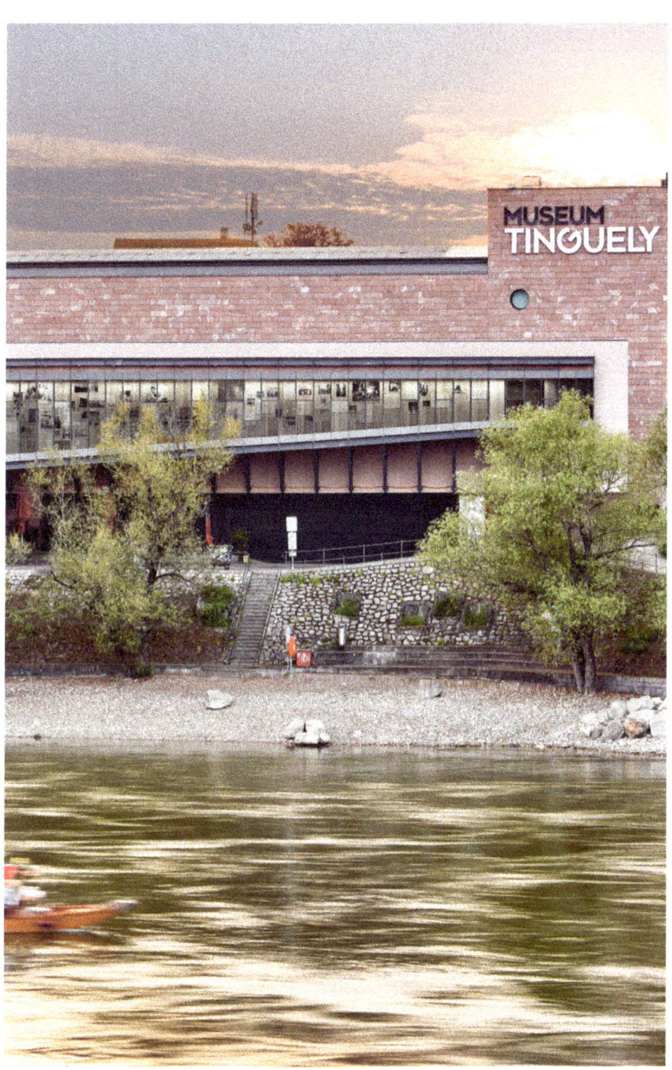
MUSEUM
TINGUELY

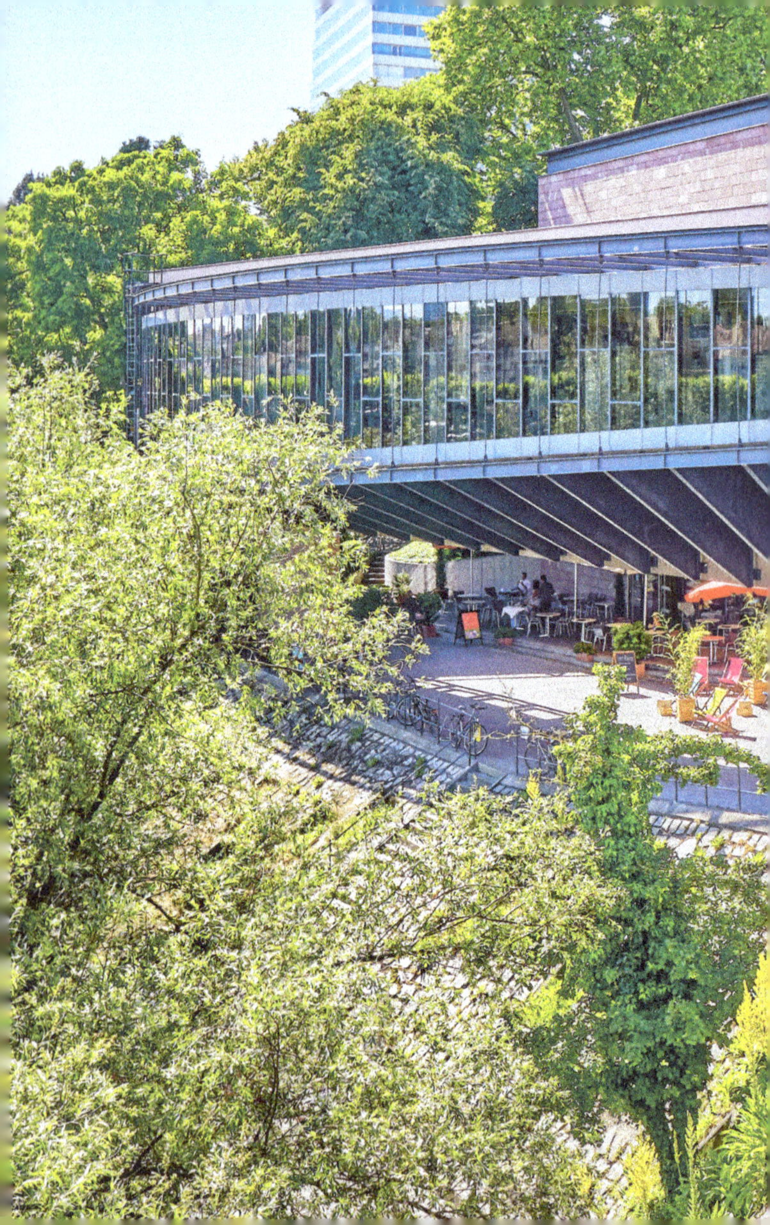

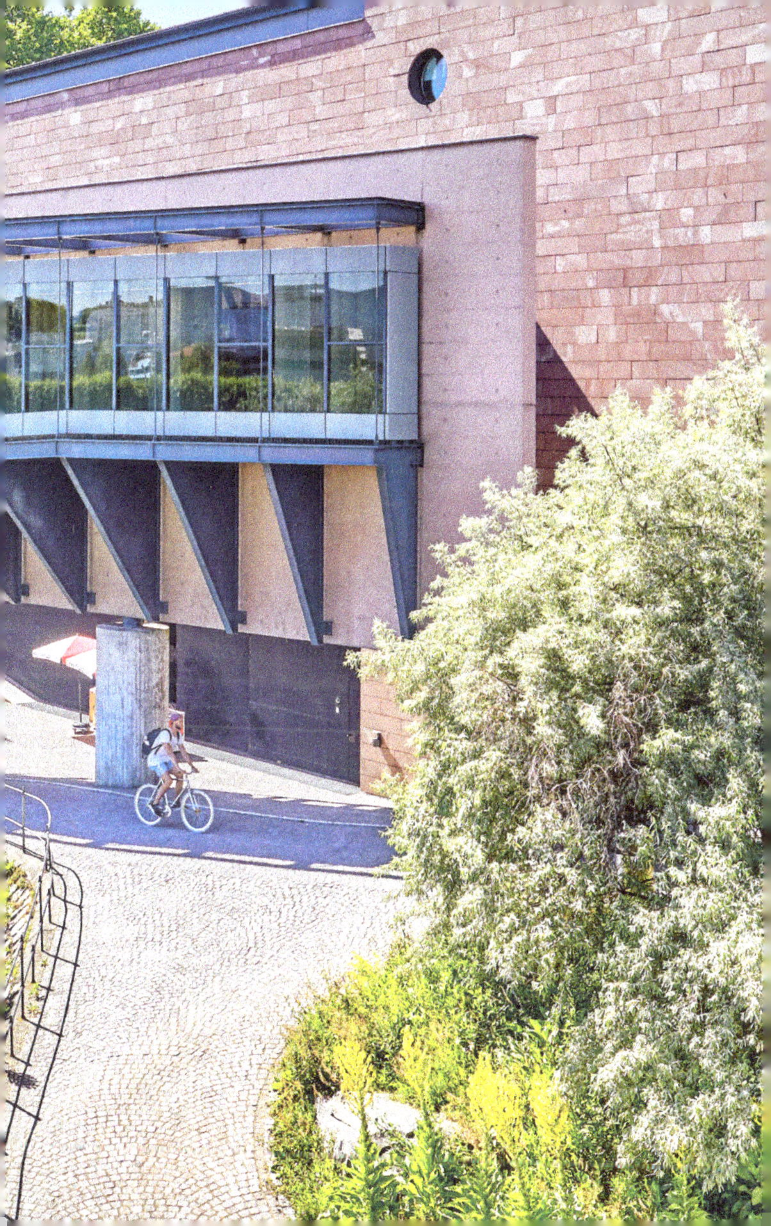

ART BASEL

— *The leading international art fair*

With its subsidiaries in Hong Kong, Paris and Miami now famous in their own right, this legendary art fair's own website calls the original "Art Basel in Basel." But while Miami consistently draws "see-and-be-seen" celebrity crowds, Basel is where the serious buyers go: around 370 galleries offer their artists' works for sale here every June. Browse Miró masters on the ground floor, while on the upper floors you can buy wonderful things, like a life-sized PixCell-Deer by Kohei Nawa. My favorite has always been the adjoining Art Unlimited section, with space for fantastic installations like Leonardo Drew's exploding heap of wood. Don't go on the weekend unless you love a huge crowd. Food options are scattered indoors and in the courtyard. There are local restaurants nearby—your ticket lets you come and go. Art Basel also includes nursing rooms if you're bringing the baby.

MESSEPLATZ 10, 4005 BASEL
ARTBASEL.COM

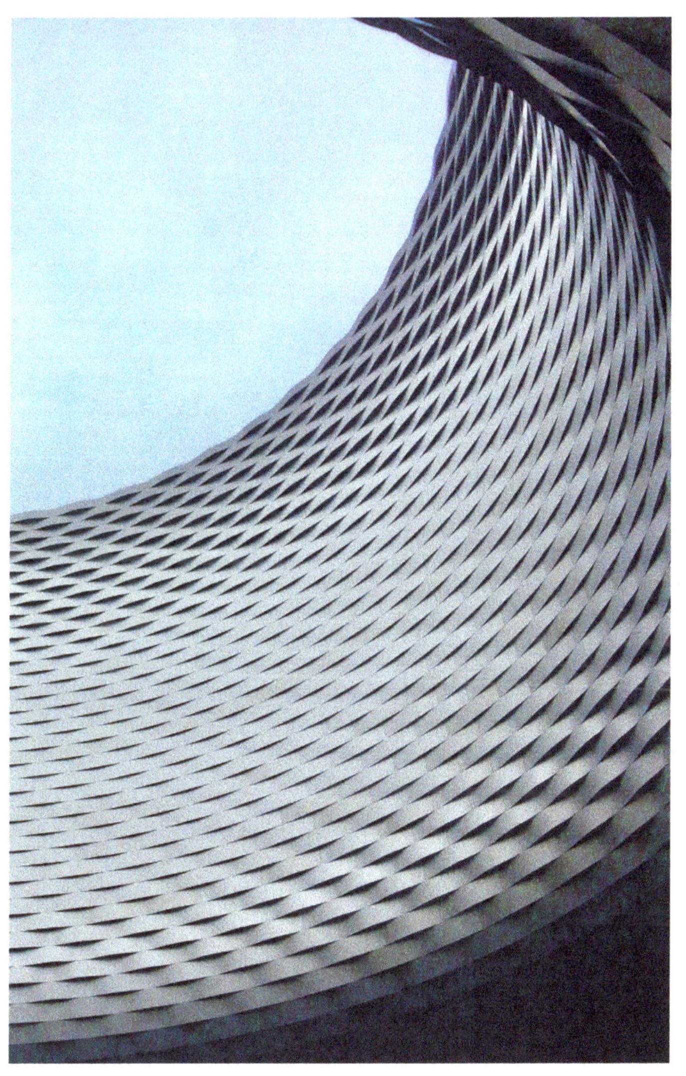

VON BARTHA

— A private gallery with drive

This is possibly the only art gallery in the world where you can fill your car with gas while you look at its window display. The pumps are left over from the space's previous incarnation as an auto mechanic's shop and now belong to the adjacent store. This Art Basel regular has been an international institution since 1970. Second-generation director Stefan von Bartha's gallery focuses on contemporary art, representing artists such as Marina Adams, Francisco Sierra, Imi Knoebel, and Sarah Oppenheimer. With engaging staff and dynamic, compelling exhibitions, von Bartha is worth regular visits. The burger joint next door, which also offers vegetarian pizzas, makes a great before-or-after pit stop.

KANNENFELDPLATZ 6, 4056 BASEL
VONBARTHA.COM

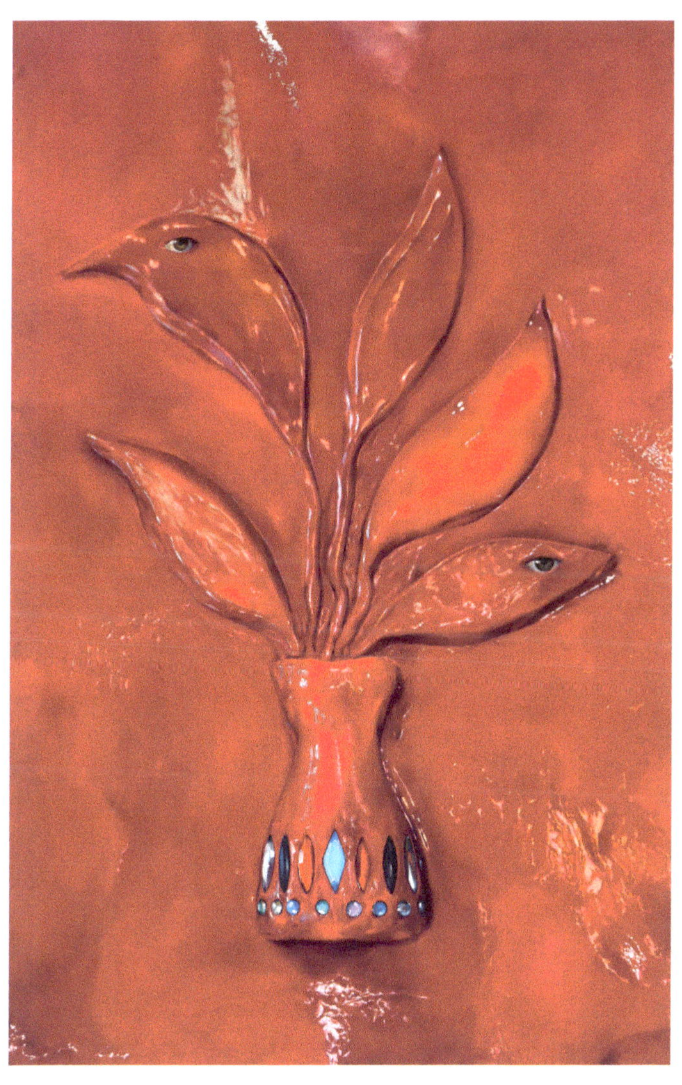

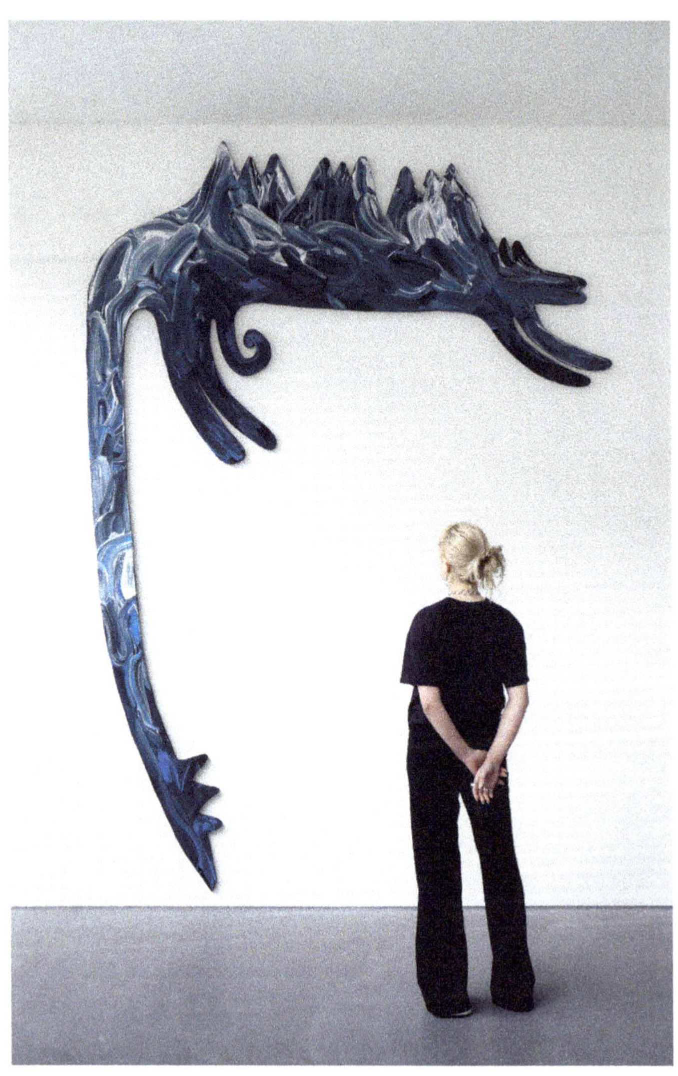

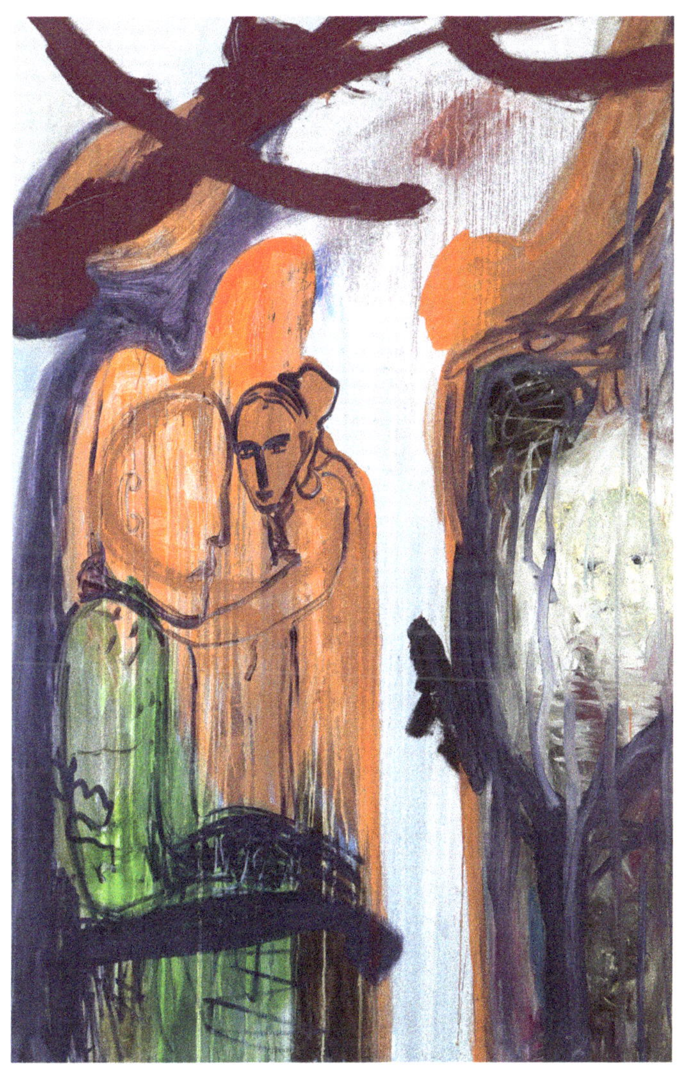

FONDATION BEYELER

— *Internationally renowned art and architecture*

Another "I'd-live-here-if-only" building: this one by Renzo Piano is low-slung and set in a gorgeous park, housing a superlative collection of art from the mid-19th century onwards. The usual suspects like Manet, Monet, Rothko, and Warhol are enhanced by the likes of Louise Bourgeois, Tacita Dean, Marlene Dumas, Jeff Wall, and Wolfgang Tillmans. The Beyeler is hugely popular, so plan on standing in line on weekends and holidays, or aim for a rainy Tuesday morning in early January. Get ahead on your Christmas shopping at what is arguably the best museum gift shop in Switzerland, which includes items designed exclusively for the Beyeler. If you can, grab a highly prized outdoor table at the adjacent Beyeler Restaurant im Park. The 18th-century villa looks over the lush gardens, with a locally sourced, seasonal menu and a wine list that will make the afternoon glide along nicely.

BASELSTRASSE 101, 4125 RIEHEN/BASEL
FONDATIONBEYELER.CH

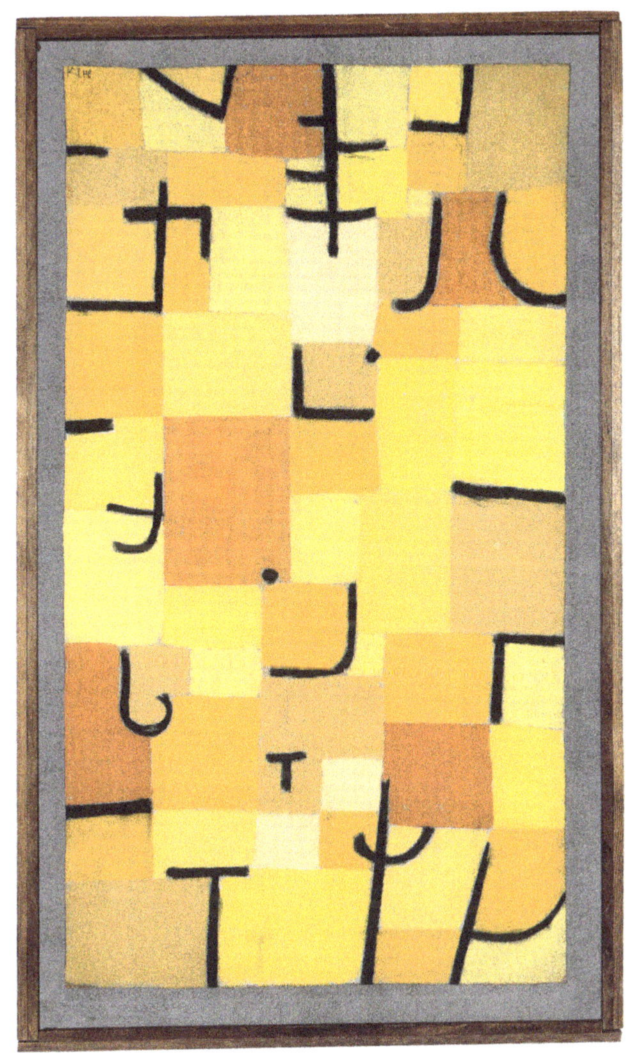

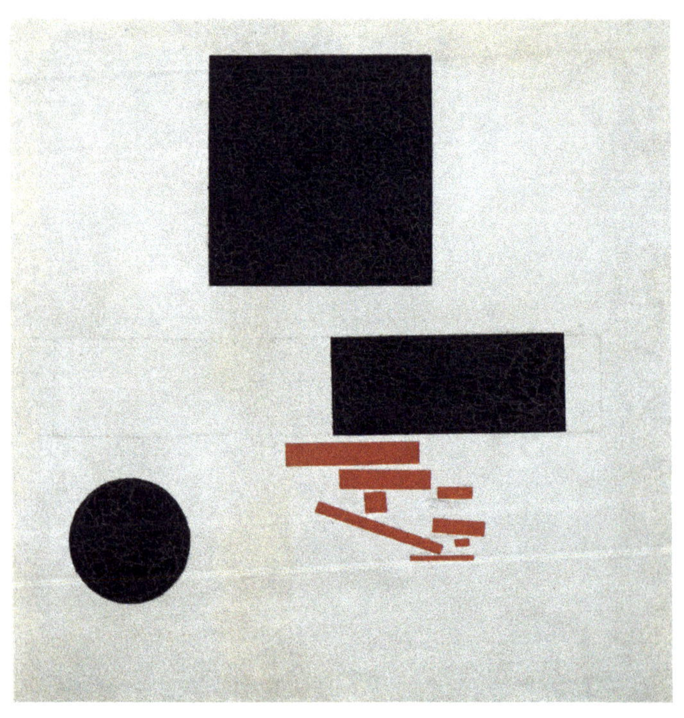

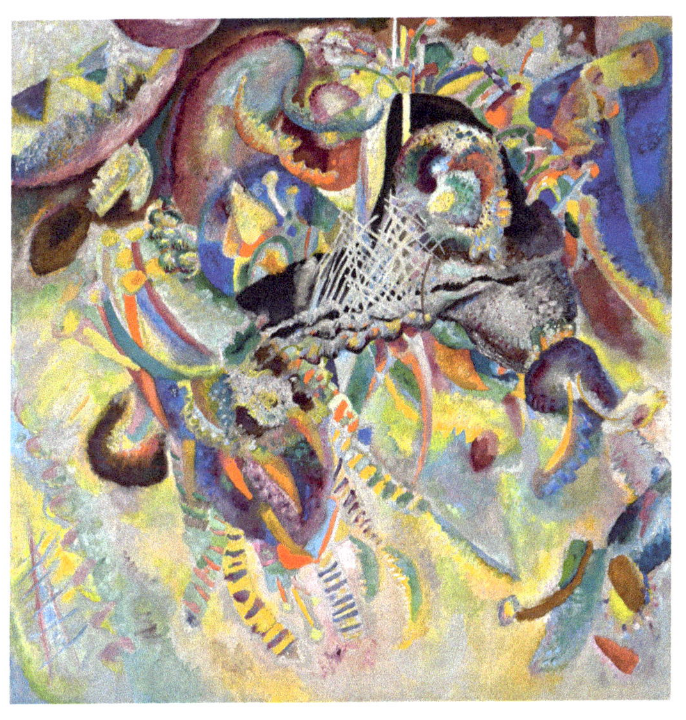

ZENTRUM PAUL KLEE

— An ode to a Swiss master

Another in a line of Swiss art museums and galleries that called on world-class architects to create a spectacular home for their collections. The museum's address references Klee's watercolor "Monument an der Grenze des Fruchtlandes" and the building by Renzo Piano runs with this concept. It has a roof in the form of an undulating wave of glass and steel with three crests: one for the Klee center's Creaviva Children's Museum, one for the administrative building and research facilities, and the middle for the actual exhibition space. The permanent collection displays some 90 works by Paul Klee that follow his experimentation with various artistic movements throughout his life. It's no wonder, then, that the artists chosen for temporary exhibitions, like Hamed Abdalla and Sarah Morris, more than succeed as reciprocal dialog with his works.

MONUMENT IM FRUCHTLAND 3, 3006 BERN
ZPK.ORG

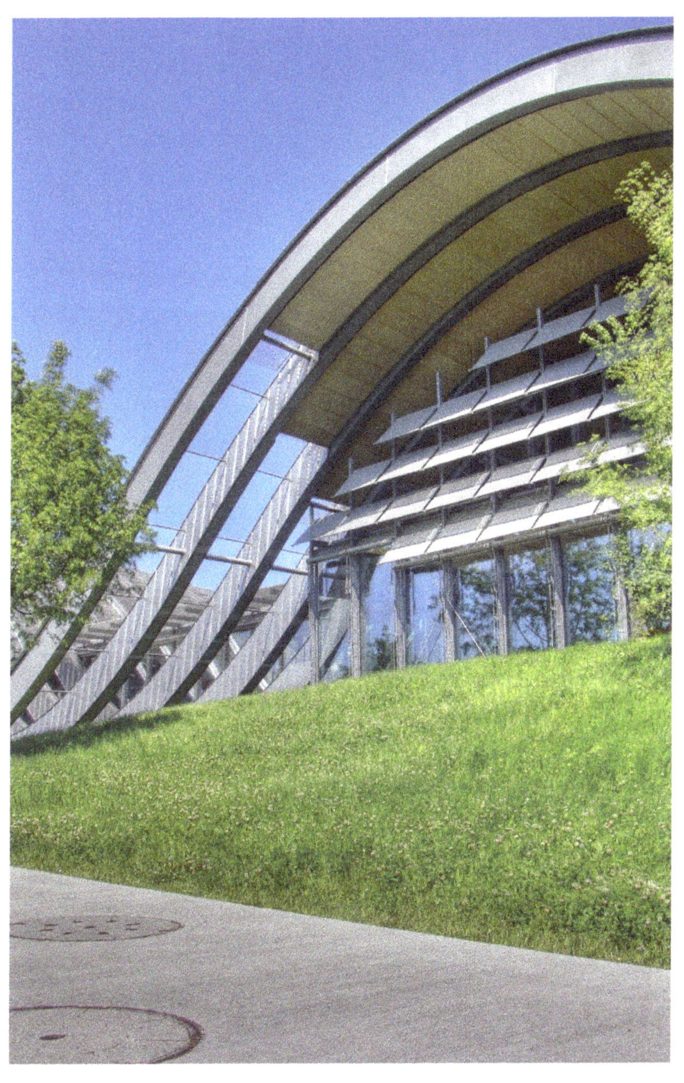

12

KUNSTHALLE BERN

— *A contemporary exhibition space with a young vibe*

The Kunsthalle Bern has been a fixed art destination since 1918, when it opened with works by 115 Bernese artists that included Cuno Amiet, Max Buri and Adèle Lilljeqvist. Its vision is dynamic and open, making a true effort to move away from the usual selection of dead, white, male artists revered elsewhere. Curators look to both local art schools and international up-and-comers for exhibitors, such as Rohini Devasher, Camilla Paolino and Eric Gyamfi, and the museum often hosts the winners of open competitions for regional artists. In warm weather, have a drink at the adjacent outdoor bar, which incorporates a huge tree that offers both shade and cover from light rain; the space is also used for readings and concerts. Gawp at the view over the Aare River to the Federal Parliament Building as you sip your drink.

HELVETIAPLATZ 1, 3005 BERN
KUNSTHALLE-BERN.CH

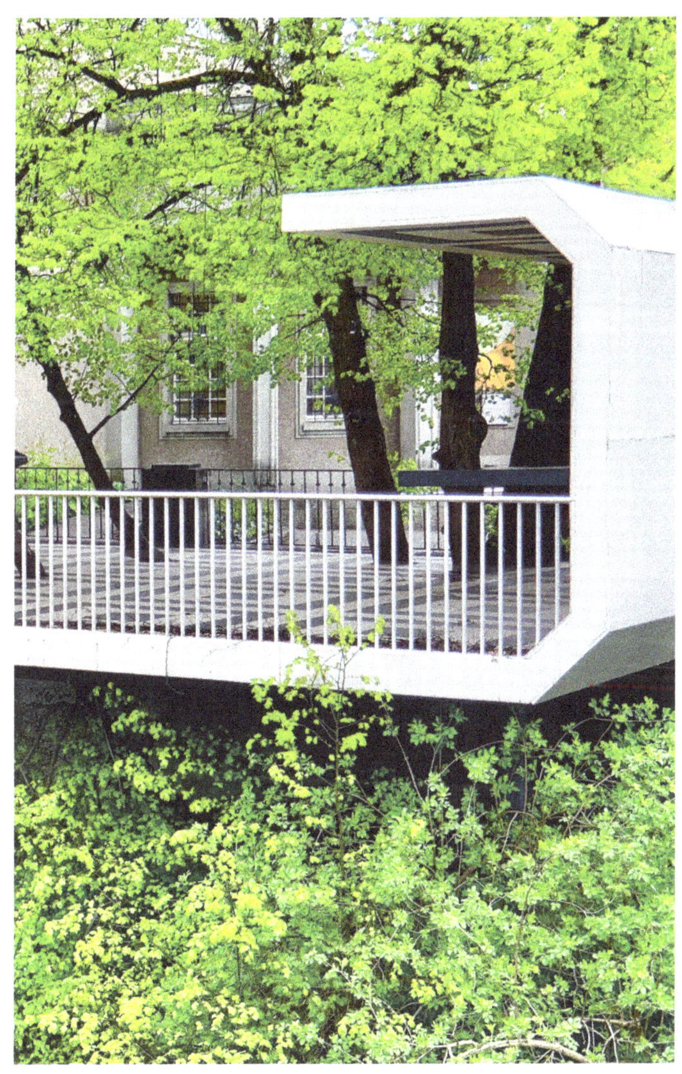

SWISS ART STATISTICS

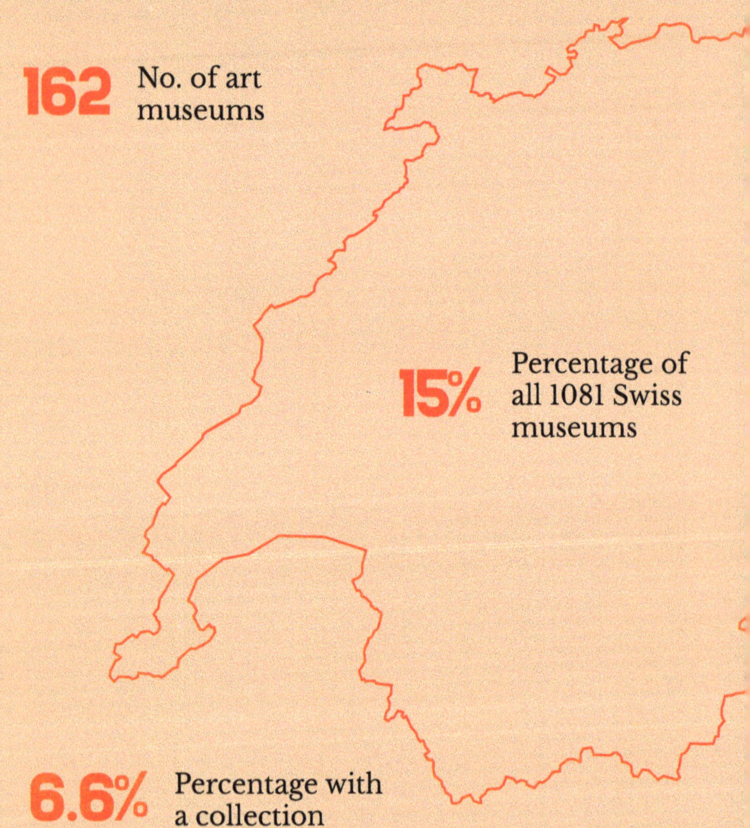

465 Average no. of exhibitions

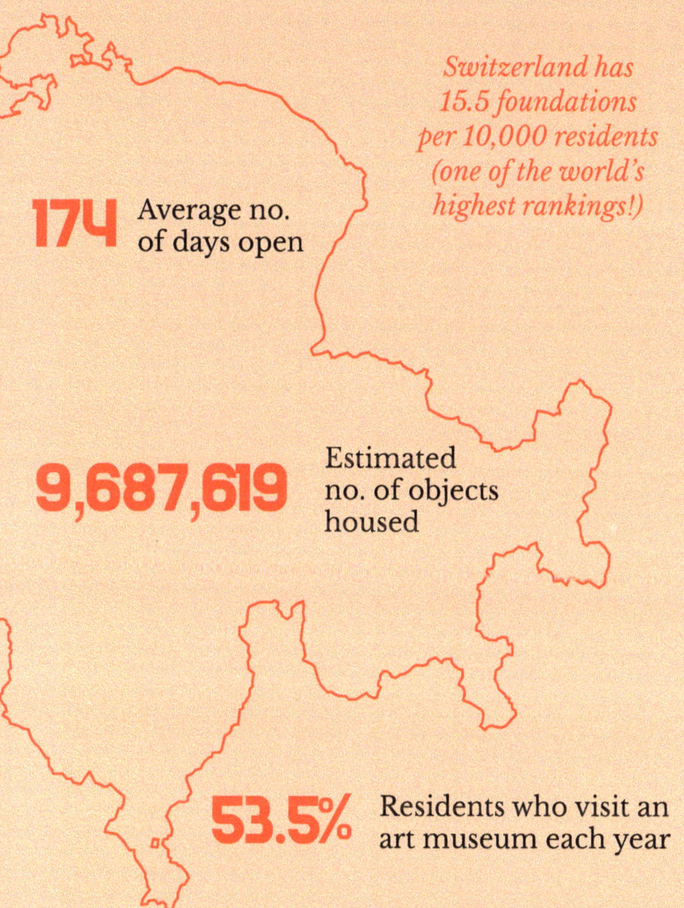

Switzerland has 15.5 foundations per 10,000 residents (one of the world's highest rankings!)

174 Average no. of days open

9,687,619 Estimated no. of objects housed

53.5% Residents who visit an art museum each year

Sources: BFS - Schweizerische Museumsstatistik 2020 and 2022 and Der Schweizer Stiftungsreport 2023.

KUNSTMUSEUM BERN

— *An art-survey course in early 20th-century Swissness*

This late 19th-century neo-renaissance structure is one of those Swiss buildings where you never know if it's a museum or a bank, and an unimposing modern addition more than doubles its size. If you're not well-versed in Swiss artists, you're in the right place: Paul Klee, Giovanni Giacometti, Ferdinand Hodler, and Meret Oppenheim are all here. There are also Dalís, Pollocks and international exhibitions, but the main focus is on the home-grown—especially from the late 19th to early 20th century. If you haven't gotten enough Klee, combine this with the fantastic Kunstmuseum Bern-affiliated Zentrum Paul Klee on the other side of town (see p.42). Go to the café late in the day: it has a machine that constantly stirs hot chocolate and by afternoon the mixture is so deliciously smooth you may decide you need your own *cioccolatiera* at home.

HODLERSTRASSE 8–12, 3011 BERN
KUNSTMUSEUMBERN.CH

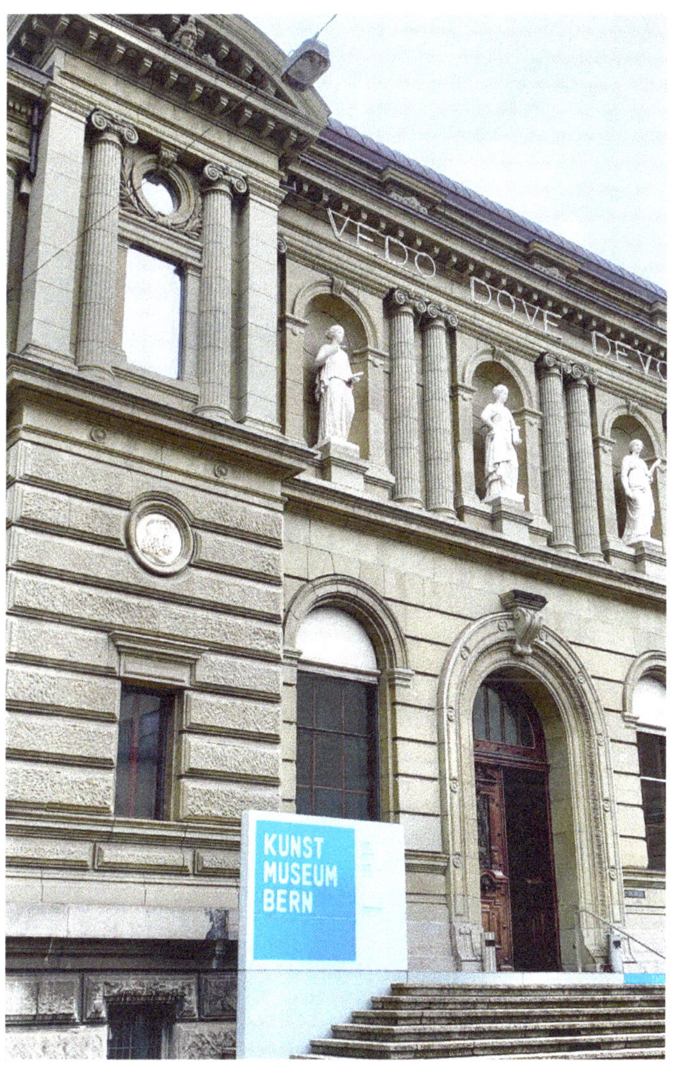
VEDO DOVE DEVO
KUNST
MUSEUM
BERN

KUNSTMUSEUM THUN

— A former grand hotel with a contemporary focus

Look up every now and then: you might be standing under an elaborately painted ceiling; then look down and admire the gorgeous parquet floors. You're standing in a repurposed 19th-century grand hotel with a large collection of local landscapes and Swiss Pop Art. These are mixed up once a year with contemporary pieces for a themed exhibition (land and cityscapes by Gustav Stettler "vs." comics by Ingo Giezendanner, paintings by Trudy Schlatter and sculptures by Leandro Bucherer, among others). Three to four exhibitions per year focus on Swiss or international contemporary artists, such as Lorna Simpson, Marguerite Saegesser and Theo Gerber. The cozy indoor Café Thunerhof (look forward to local cakes and fruit tarts) has an extra belle epoque vibe when the weather allows: tables (with blankets if necessary) on the long, covered outdoor terrace offer postcard views of the Aare River and the local Alps.

HOFSTETTENSTRASSE 14, 3602 THUN
KUNSTMUSEUMTHUN.CH

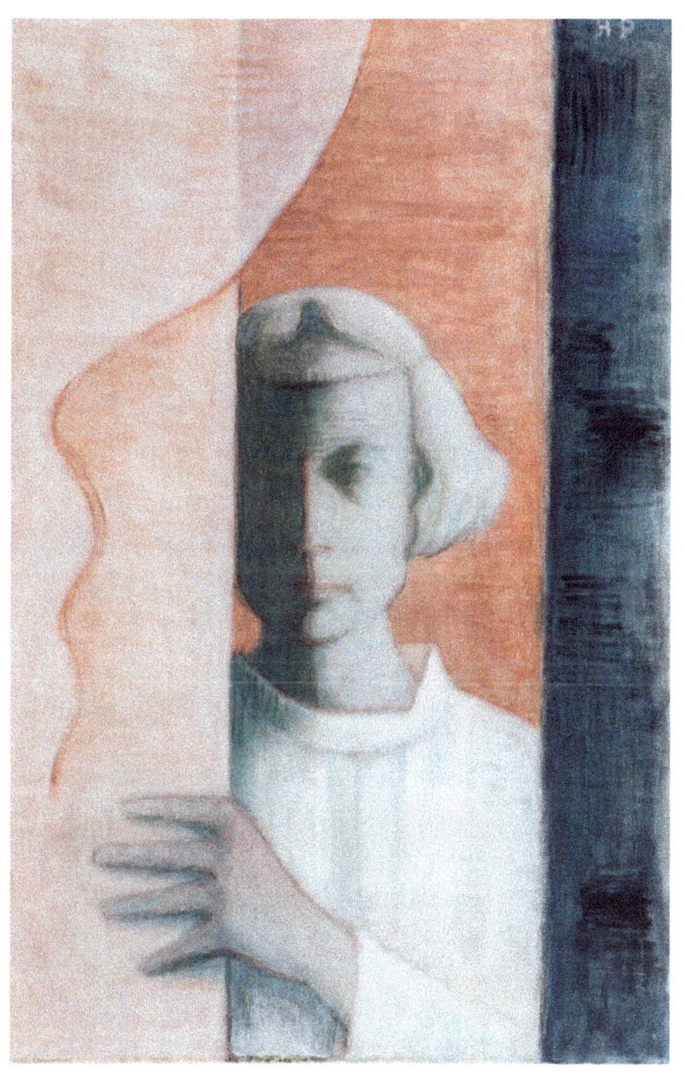

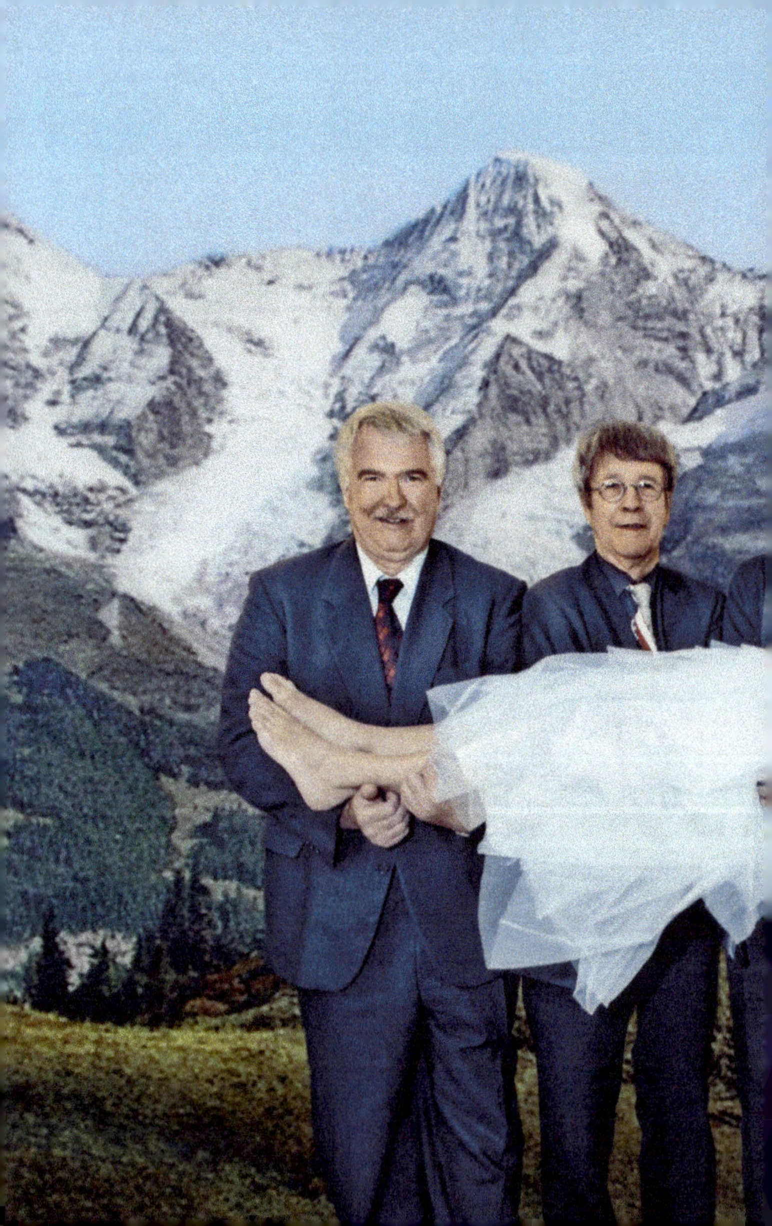

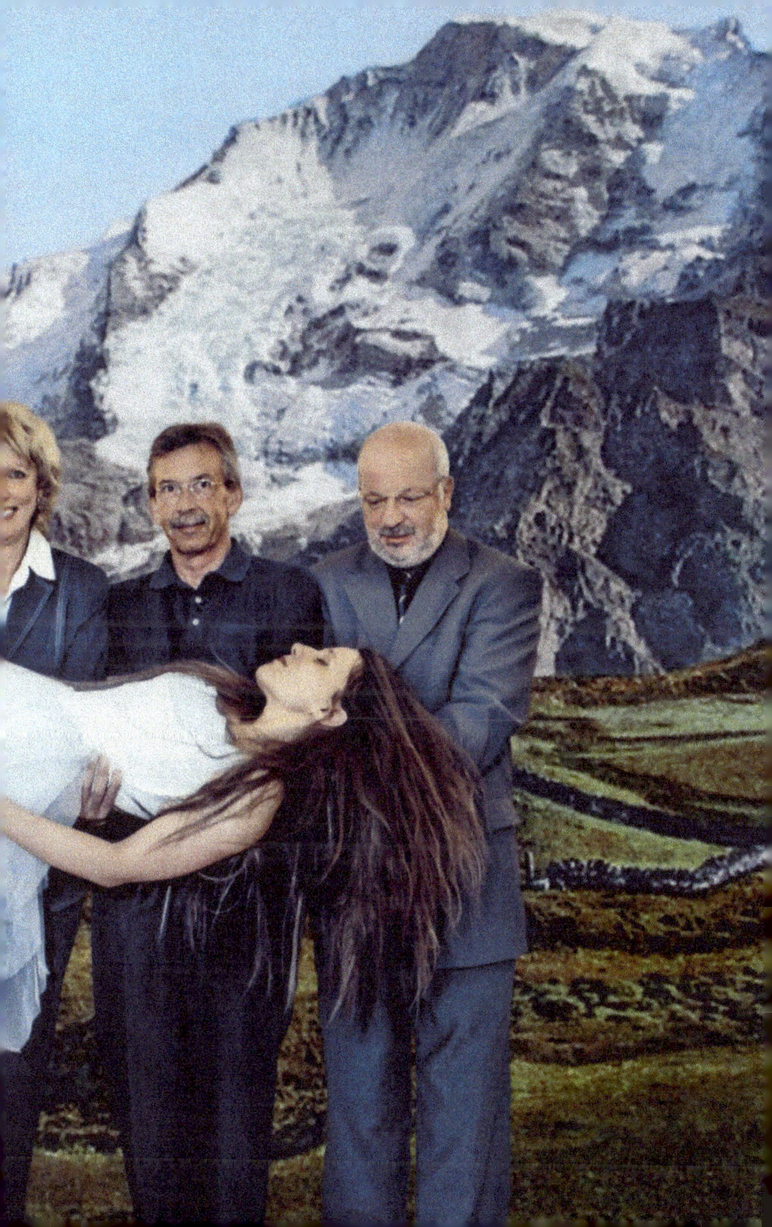

MUSÉE D'ART ET D'HISTOIRE DE GENÈVE

— *A grande dame on the edge of Geneva's old town*

Surely inspired by the Louvre in Paris, this chunk of neoclassicism, completed in 1910, has an entrance and palatial staircases that would make Louis XIV feel at home. In contrast, the actual exhibition rooms are somewhat smaller in scale, but nevertheless impress with their capacity for, say, Flemish, Italian Baroque and French Renaissance masters in enormous gilded frames. It also features cheeky modern installations, like marble runs speeding through holes in Warhol copies by Wim Delvoye, and the actual interior walls of the 17th-century Salis Castle in Zizers which was recently converted into private apartments. The MAH's offering is rounded out by antiquities, archaeological finds, graphic arts, watches, jewelry, and enamels. There is a charming café on the ground floor with access to an outdoor courtyard that serves great lunches and cakes, but falls short on the coffee.

RUE CHARLES-GALLAND 2, 1206 GENEVA
MAHMAH.CH

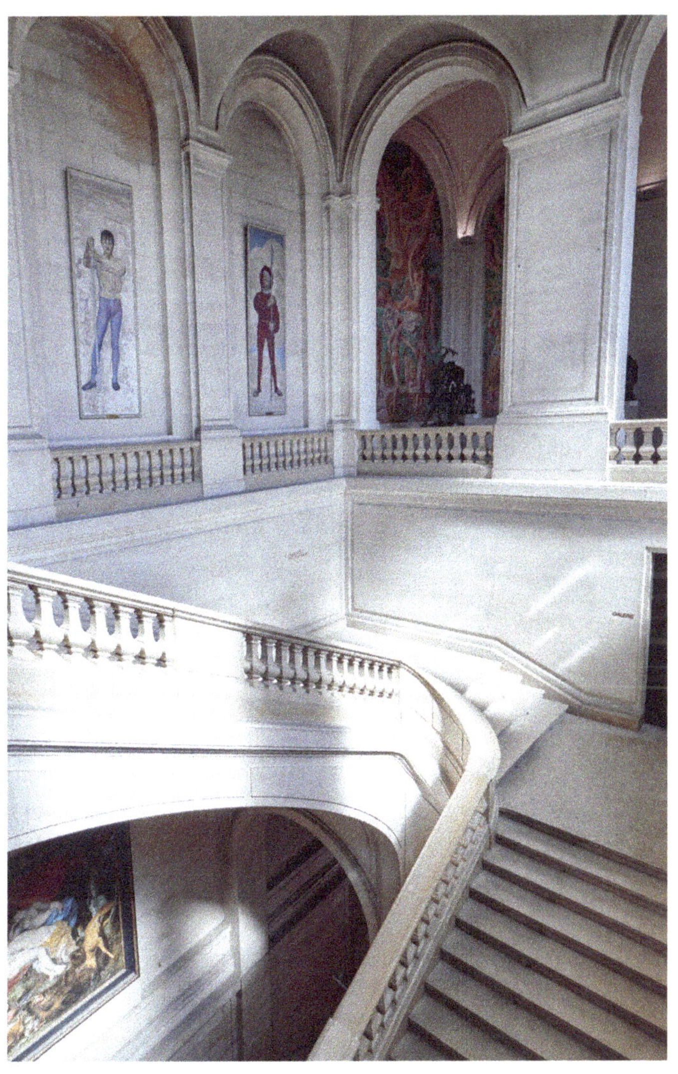

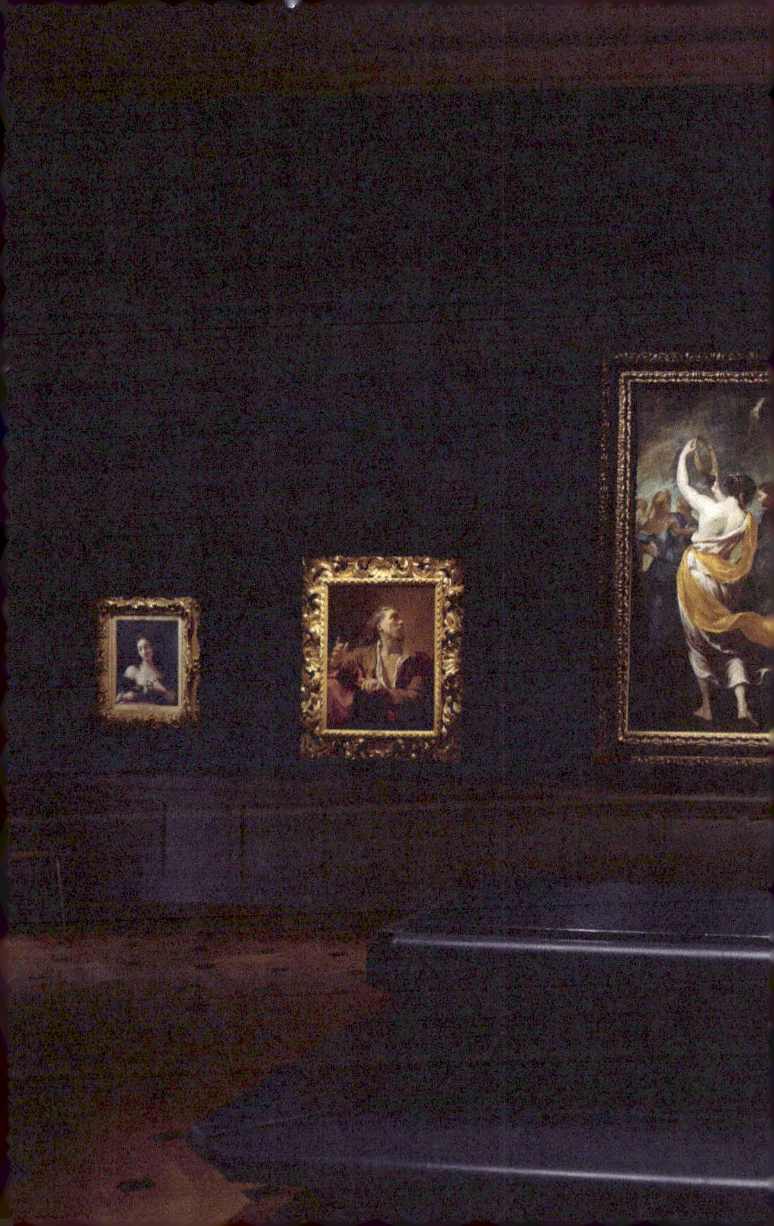

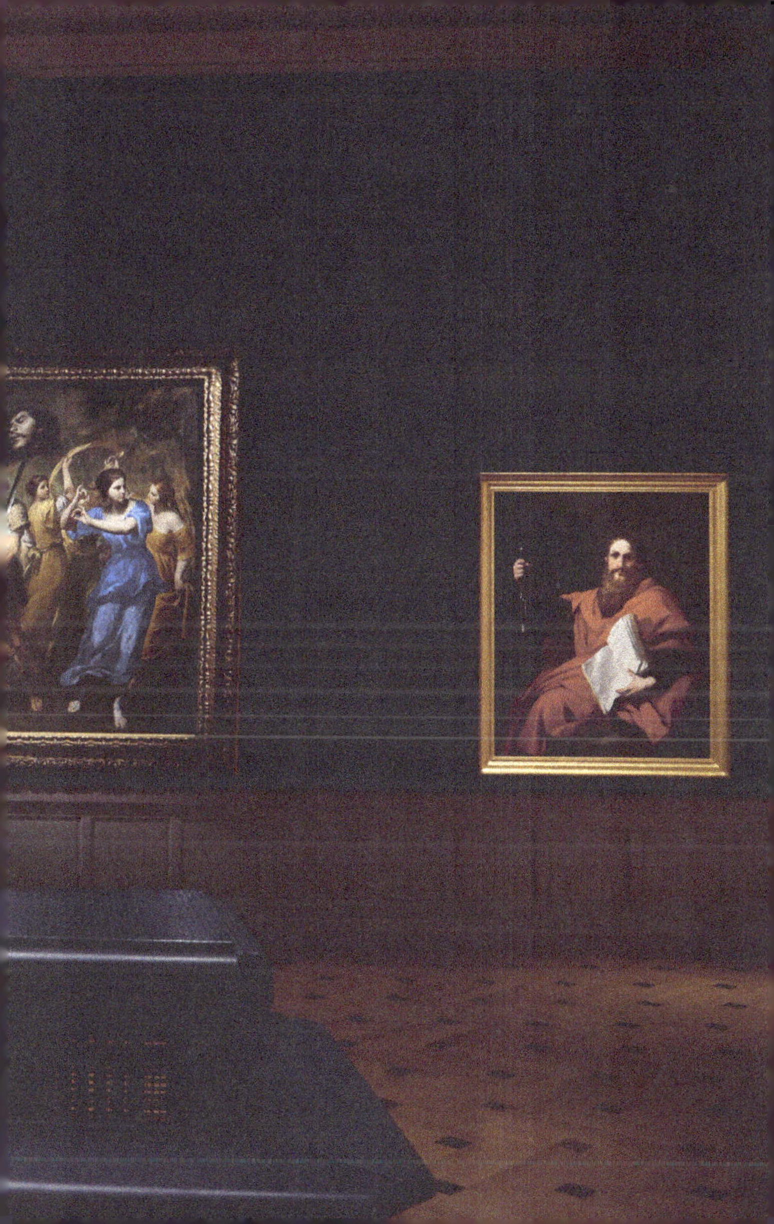

PORTS FRANCS ET ENTREPÔTS DE GENÈVE

— *The art you'll probably never see*

Geneva Freeport was established in 1888 as a duty-free transit storage facility for things like grain. Over 135 years later, it's definitely no longer about the grain, as investors have long taken notice of the freeport's advantageous conditions. Art is being parked there by collectors until the value increases. How much art? Guesses vary from US$100–400 billion, but only the tight-lipped Swiss customs office would know for sure. Dealers rent space for what are essentially tax-exempt indoor galleries. A sale often just means moving art from one storage unit to another once the money has changed hands. So, technically, you could make a gallery appointment, but you'd have to be a serious buyer. Or one of the many journalists who write about it. Or a member of the European Parliament Think Tank, which released a study in 2018 titled "Money laundering and tax evasion risks in free ports."

RTE DU GRAND-LANCY 6A, 1211 GENEVA
GENEVA-FREEPORTS.CH

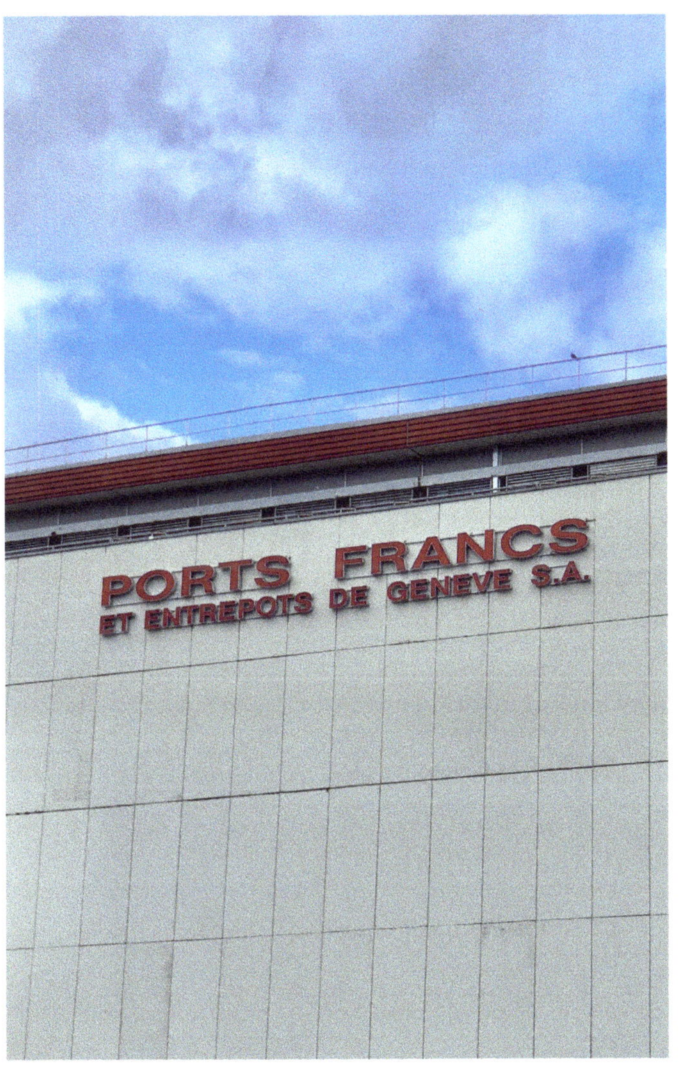
PORTS FRANCS
ET ENTREPOTS DE GENEVE S.A.

GENEVA GALLERIES

If you're looking to buy art, there's no excuse for coming home empty-handed from Geneva. The center of town is dotted with galleries of all price ranges and degrees of swankiness, so you can get anything from Ancient Greek sculptures or Gentileschis to the latest by Charlotte Herzig or Feng Xiao-Min.

1. Wilde Gallerie
2. Galerie Alexandre Mottier
3. Bel Air Fine Art
4. Galerie Renaissance
5. Galerie Polomarco
6. Calamart
7. Gowen Contemporary
8. Mabe Gallery
9. Galerie Schifferli
10. Galerie Sonia Zannettacci
11. Opera Gallery
12. Bailly Gallery
13. Gagosian Gallery
14. Salomon Lilian
15. Phoenix Ancient Art
16. Young Collectors by Phoenix Ancient Art
17. Patrick Gutknecht Gallery
18. Espace Muraille

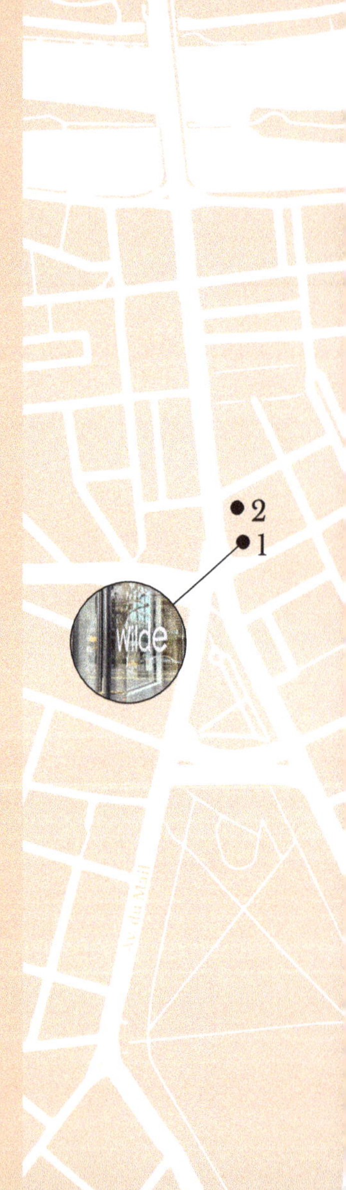

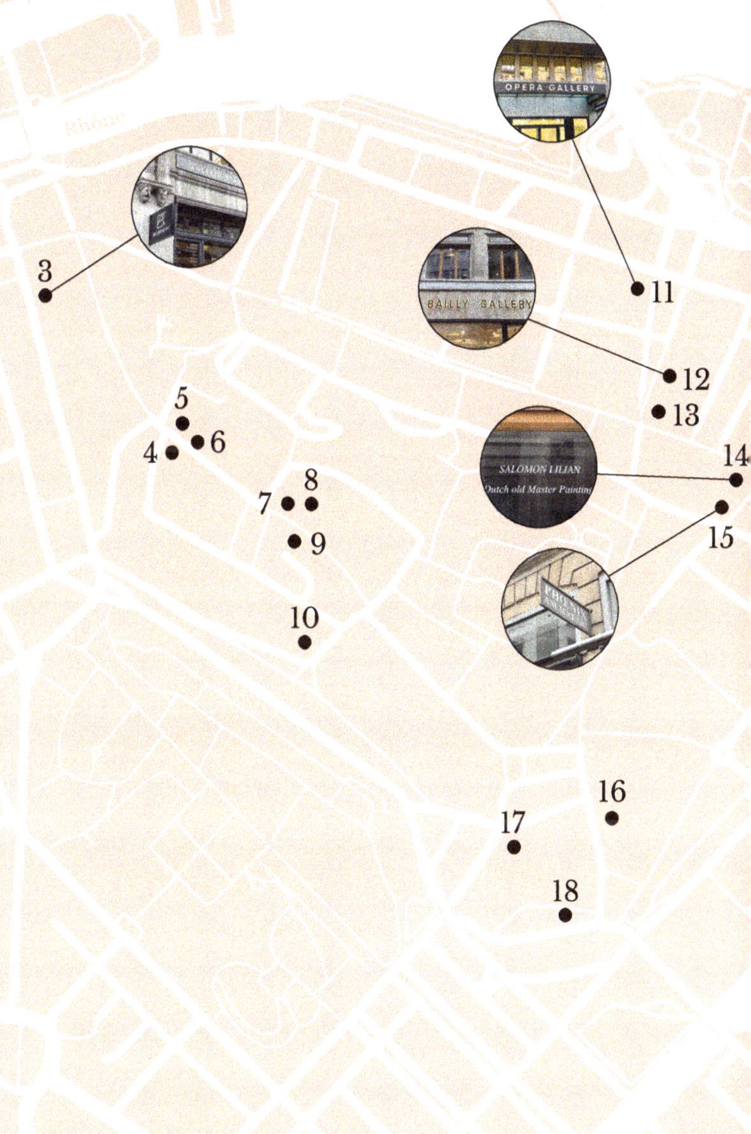
Rhône
OPERA GALLERY
BAILLY GALLERY
SALOMON LILIAN
Dutch old Master Painting
3
4
5
6
7
8
9
10
11
12
13
14
15
16
17
18

BÜNDNER KUNSTMUSEUM CHUR

— *A stately 19th-century villa and a three-story white cube*

What unites two seemingly unconnected buildings—one historical, one modern—is that they make up the Bündner Kunstmuseum Chur; they are indeed also physically connected by the basement exhibition space. A collection founded on pieces acquired in 1900 now stretches from the 18th century to the present. Highlights are the three rooms dedicated to the Giacomettis—Giovanni, Alberto, Diego, and Augusto—as well as two rooms for Angelica Kauffman. Born in Chur, this Swiss Neoclassical portrait and "history" painter moved to London, where she was a founding member of the prestigious Royal Academy of Arts, and Rome, where she lies buried in the Basilica Sant'Andrea delle Fratte. Do not miss sampling the homemade tortes in the villa's award-winning café.

BAHNHOFSTRASSE 35, 7000 CHUR
KUNSTMUSEUM.GR.CH

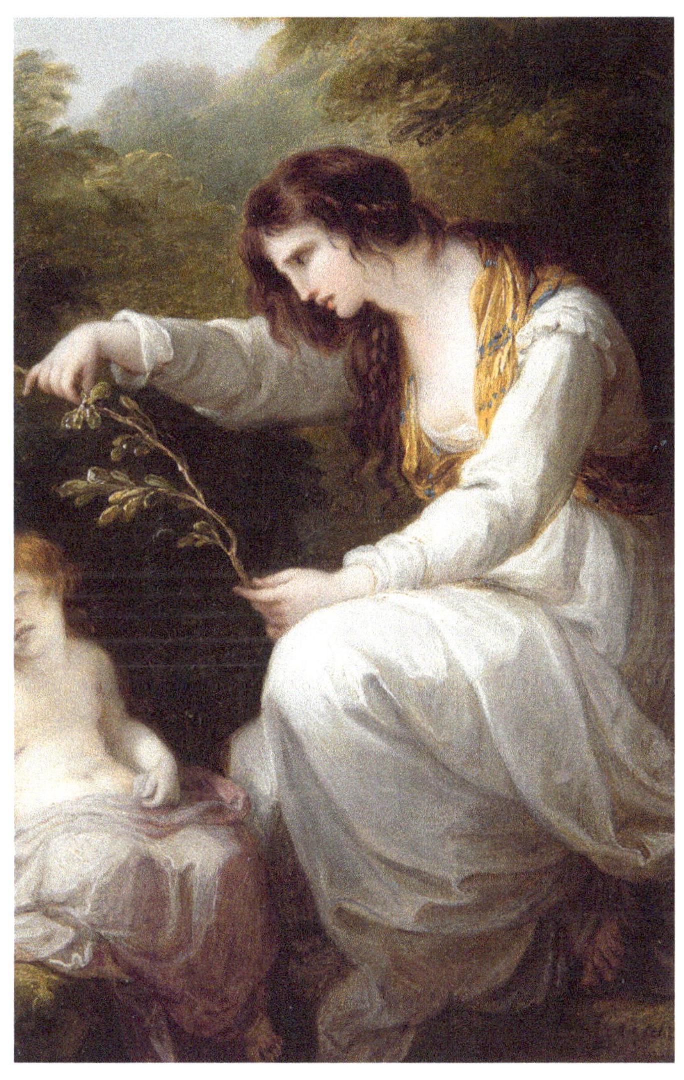

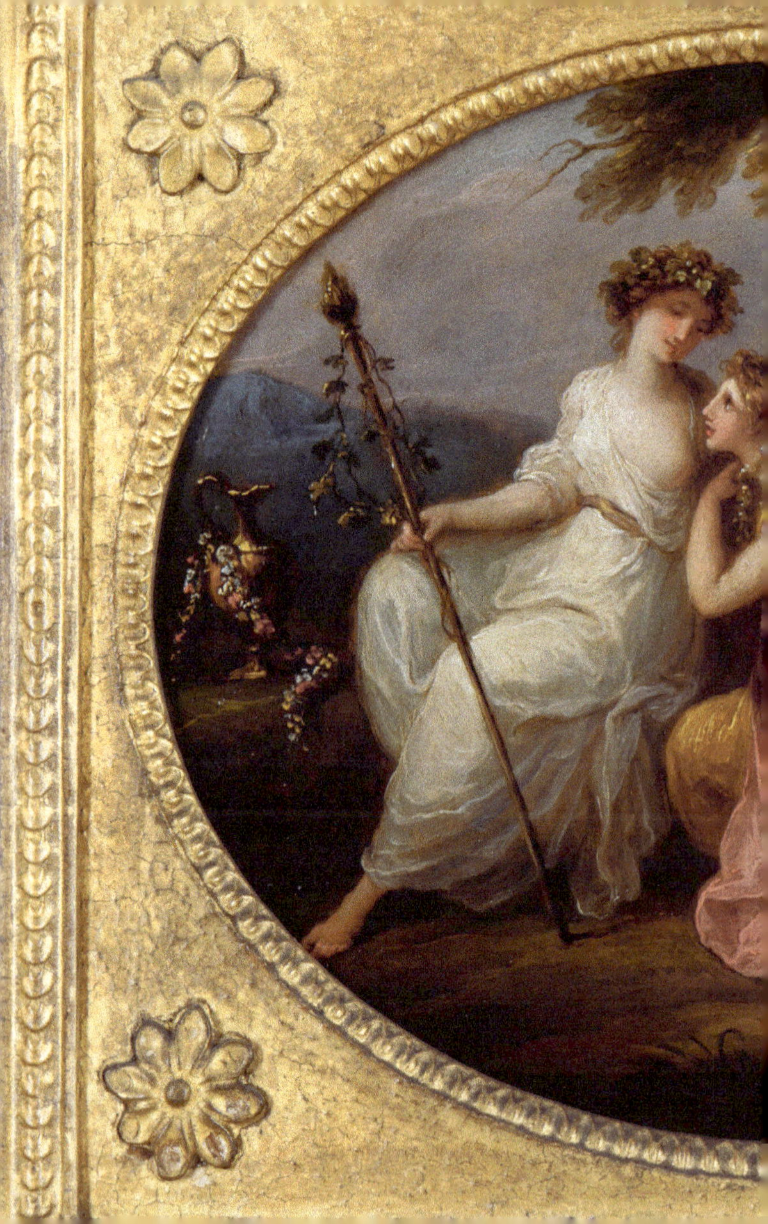

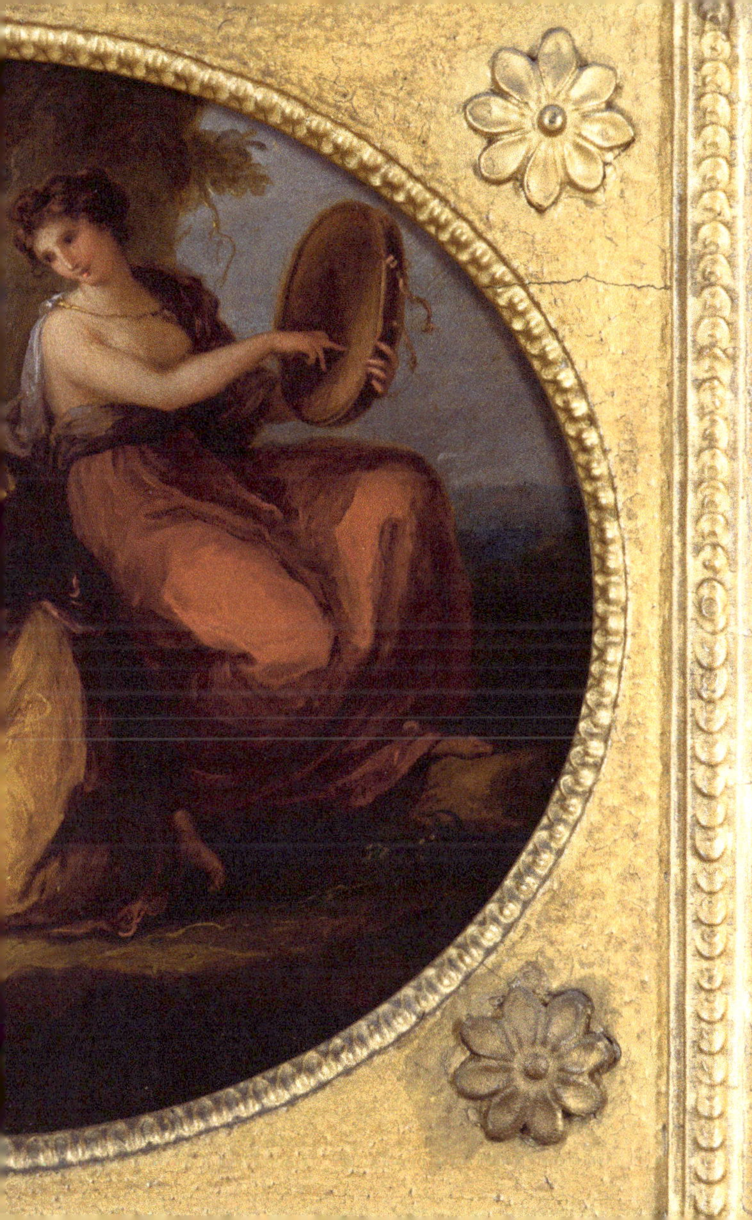

MUZEUM SUSCH

— *The female gaze*

Founded in 2019 by Polish entrepreneur Grażyna Kulczyk, the predominant focus of Muzeum Susch is on artwork by women, such as Magdalena Abakanowicz and Monika Sosnowska—a refreshing take in the testosterone-laden art world. From the outside, the museum looks like what it used to be: a collection of renovated monastic buildings—vicarage, hospice, breweries (yes, plural)—in a quiet little Alpine town of 200. For the interior, imagine a stylish rabbit warren inside Hermione Granger's bag. Some rooms are timbered in Swiss pine, while others are underground caves, blasted out by engineers who removed 9000 metric tons of rock to triple the exhibition space to 1500 m². The cave system, which links the museum's four buildings together, is definitely easier on those with sturdy knees (only parts are wheelchair accessible), but worth a few hours of hiking 169 steps up and down from room to astonishing room.

SURPUNT 78, 7542 SUSCH
MUZEUMSUSCH.CH

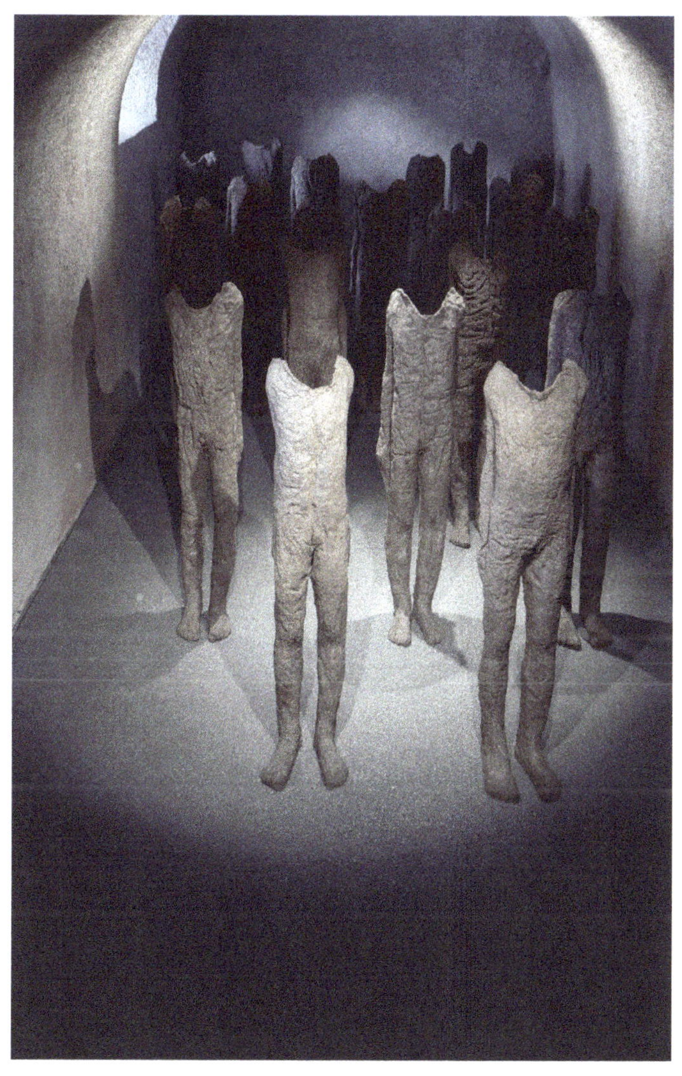

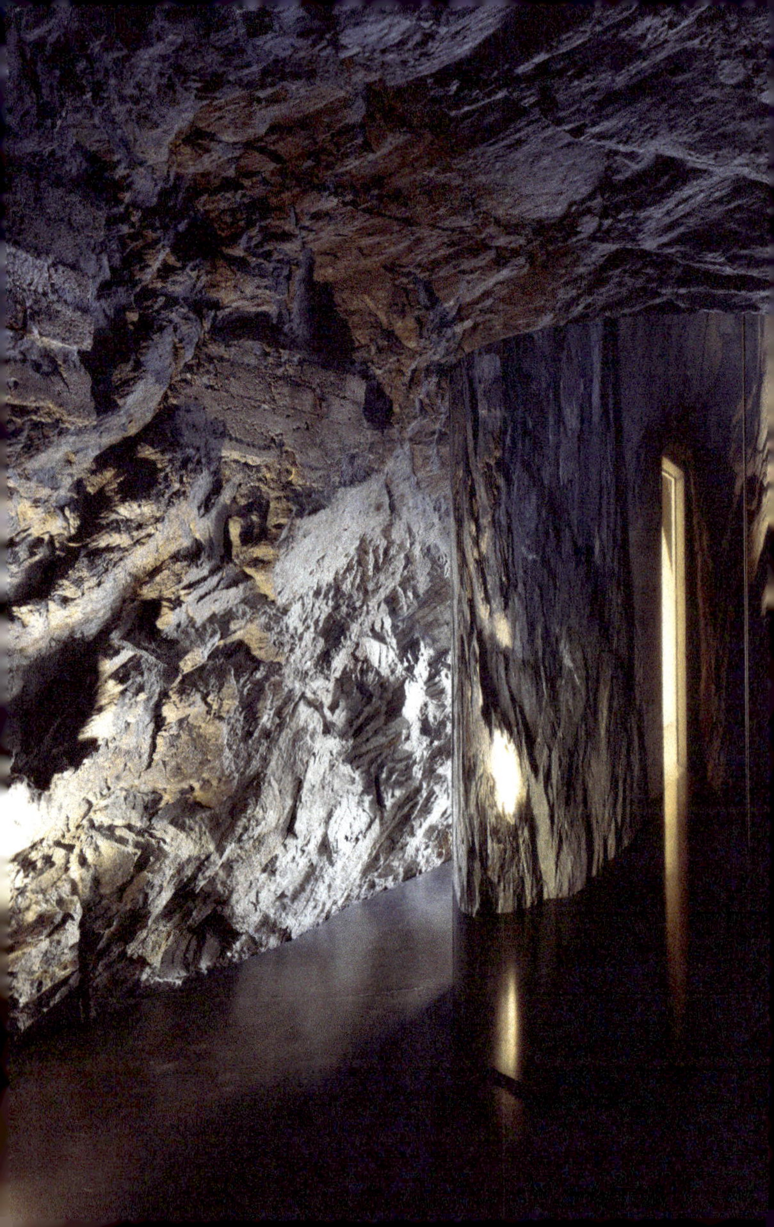

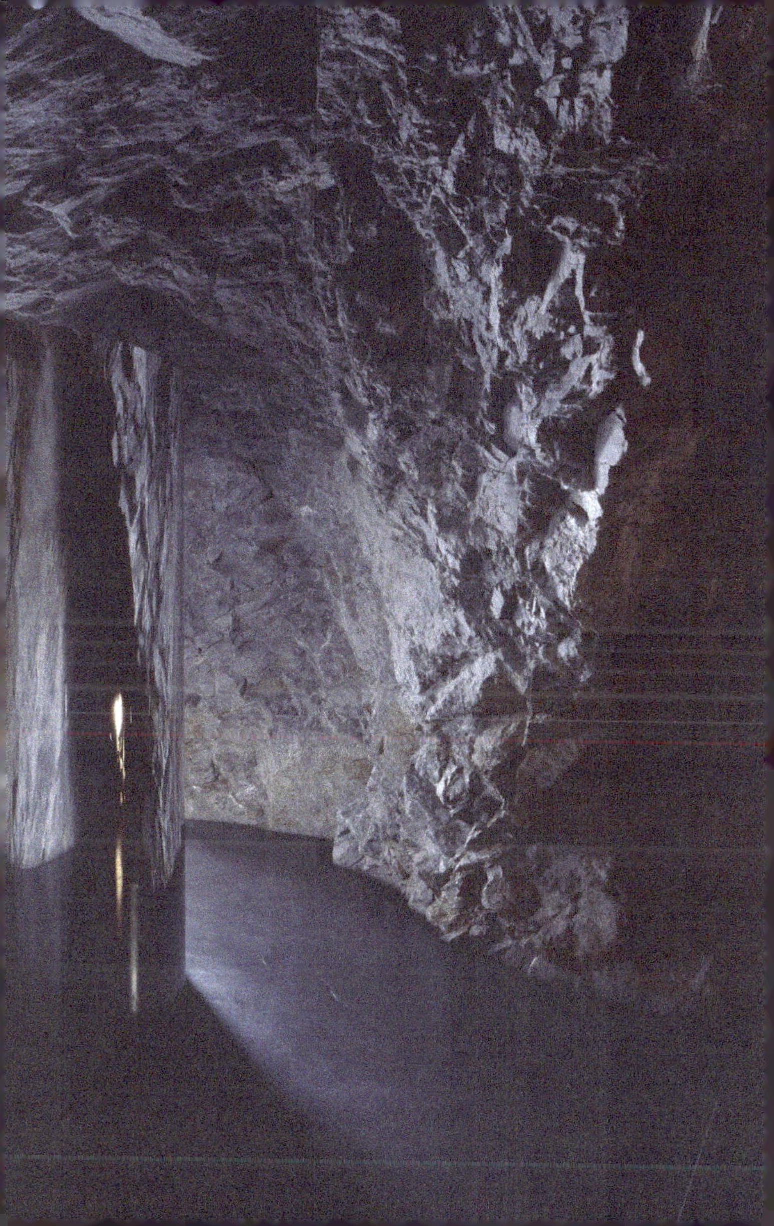

19

SAMMLUNG ROSENGART

— *Lucerne's modern art mecca*

Imagine running an art gallery and counting Pablo Picasso, who makes portraits of you over 12 years, as a personal friend. Imagine buying and falling in love with the works of Paul Klee at a time when no one was interested in him, so you keep them for yourself. Then you add more of your favorites, from Camille Pissarro to Vassily Kandinsky. This is how Angela Rosengart and her father, Siegfried, amassed a substantial private collection of over 320 works over 50 years. In 2002, it opened as the Sammlung Rosengart in a former bank on prime real estate in downtown Lucerne. The collection is spread over three floors: one dedicated to Klee, one to Picasso and one to the rest of the modernists. If you're not big on crowds, you can book the museum for a private tour and add a flying buffet for up to 50 friends.

PILATUSSTRASSE 10, 6003 LUCERNE
ROSENGART.CH

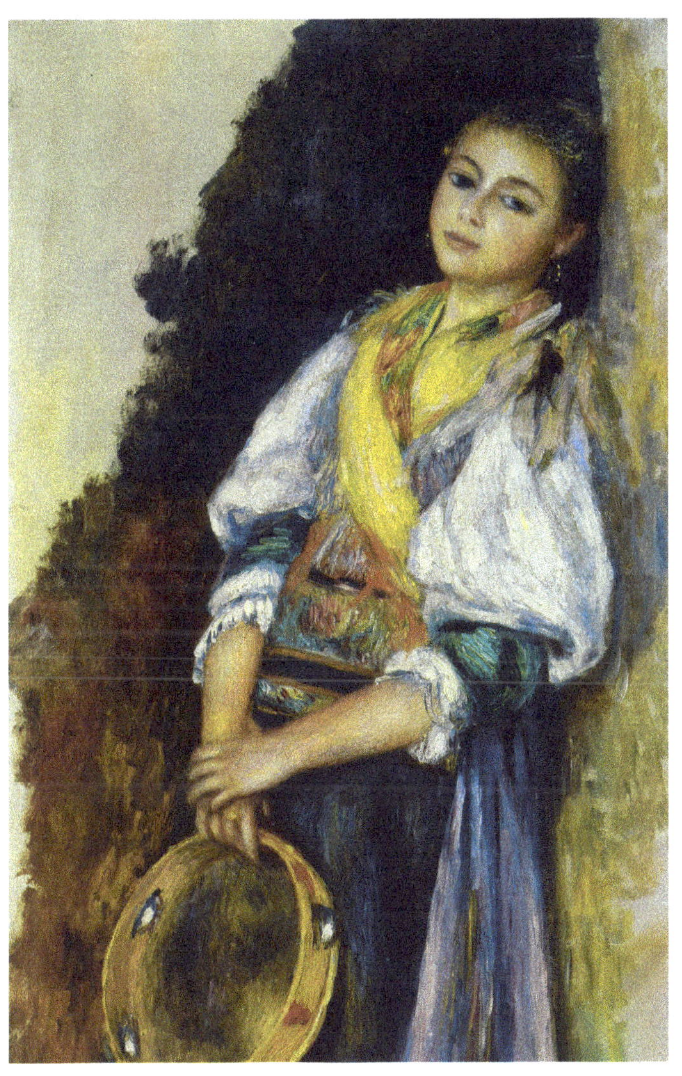

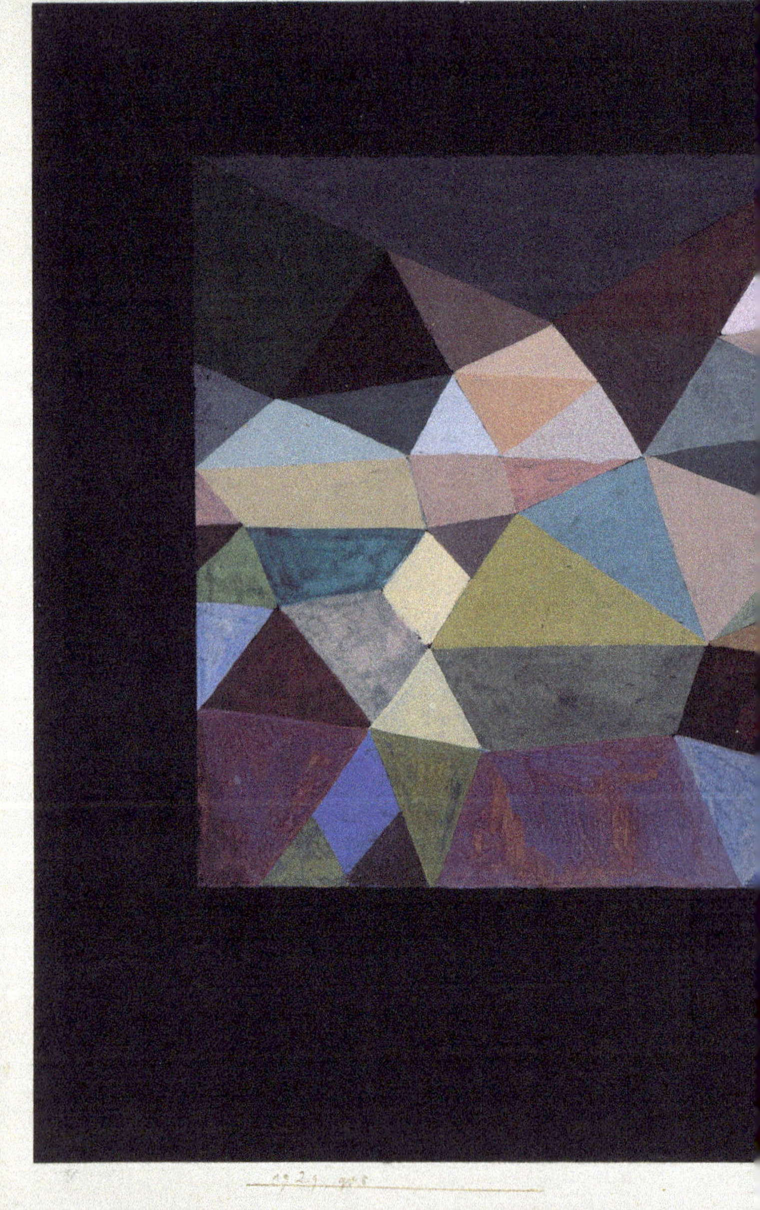

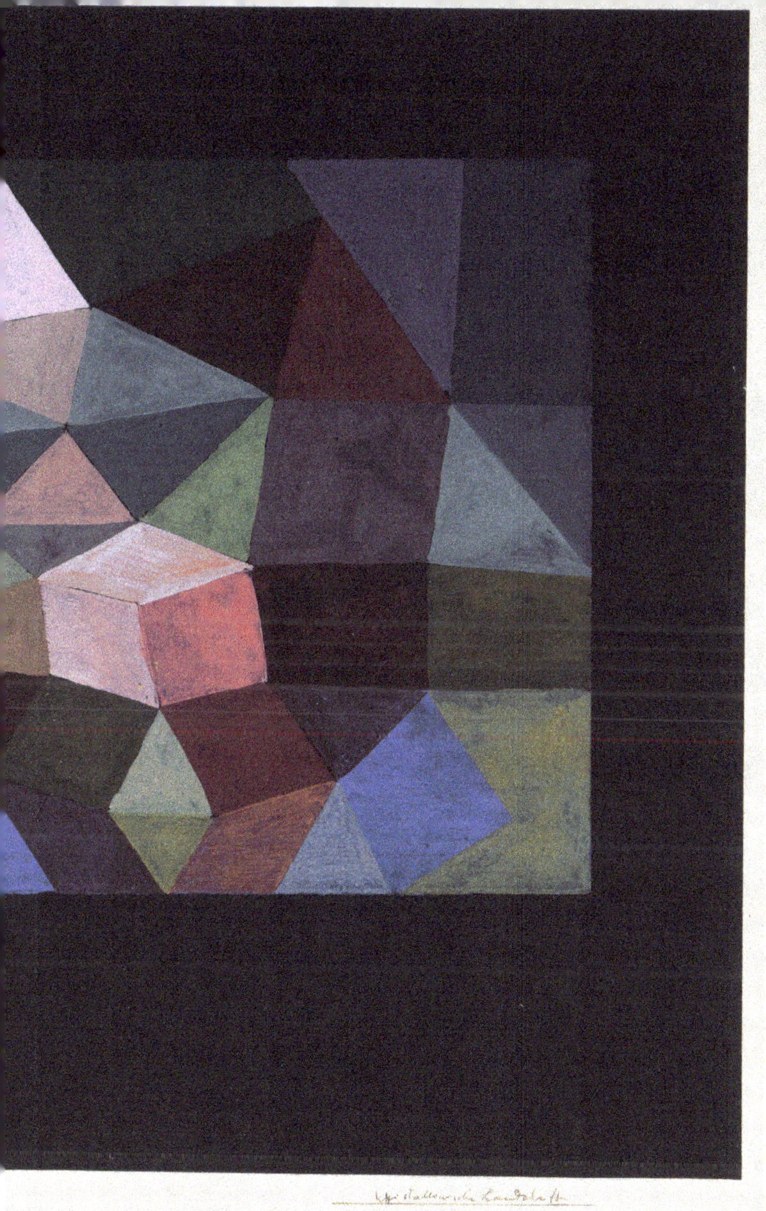

KUNSTMUSEUM SOLOTHURN

— *Masters and Swiss contemporaries converse*

Not one to hang its art in strict historical order, this free-admission municipal museum is a great place to discover pieces you'd possibly overlook in other venues. If you tend to skip the medieval section because you're not generally a fan of religious paintings, you may look at them differently once they're hanging next to a contemporary video installation or are part of an exhibition arranged by subject. The curators are always finding new ways to mix up the collection of mainly Swiss art, including Hodler and Amiet, and 16th-to-20th-century masters, such as Holbein and Matisse; you never know what's around the corner. The museum's commitment to contemporary Swiss artists is reflected by regular solo exhibitions, too. The refreshment counter is limited to a good espresso machine and a few packaged local snacks, but there are excellent restaurants nearby if you're really hungry.

WERKHOFSTRASSE 30, 4500 SOLOTHURN
KUNSTMUSEUM-SO.CH

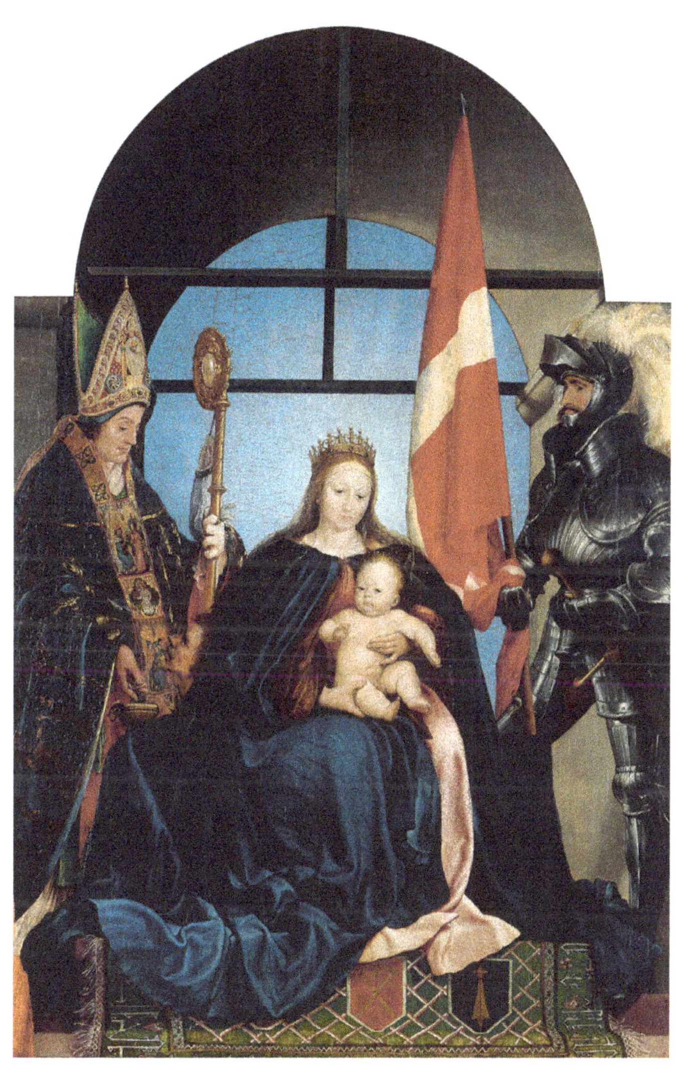

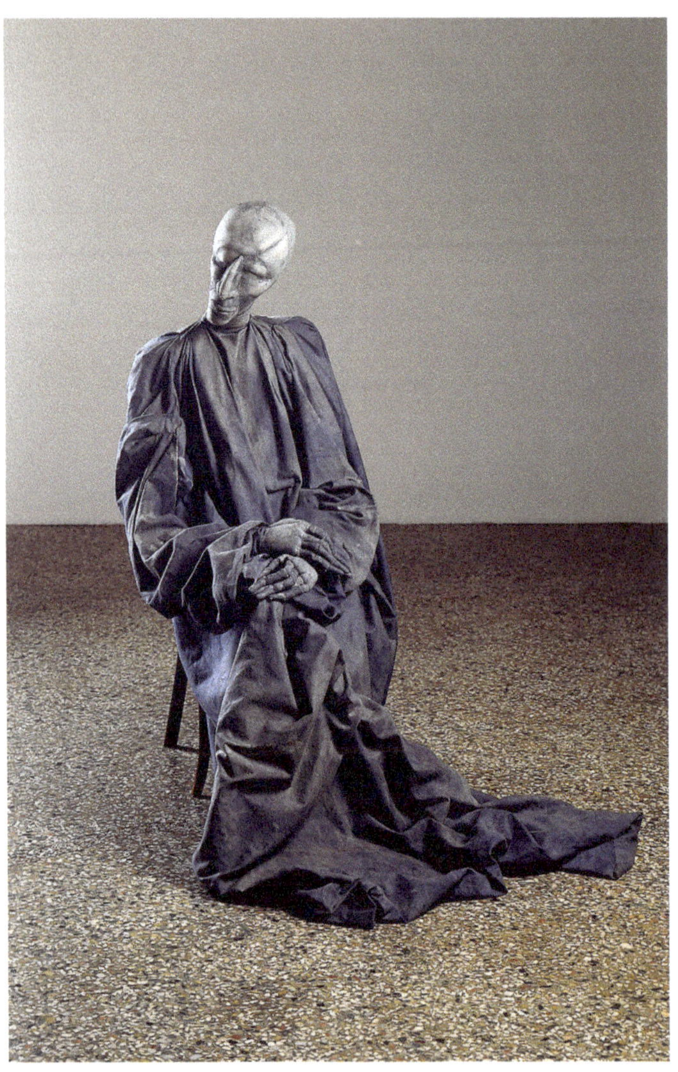

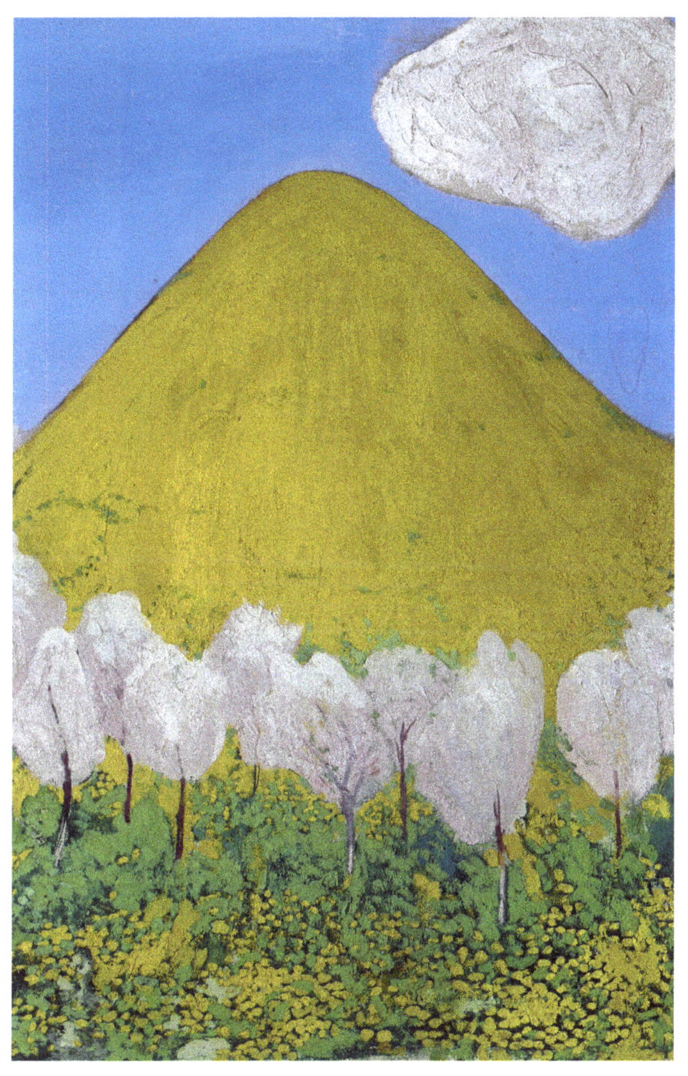

SWISS ART PATRONS

The Swiss private sector, in the form of industrialists, architects, archaeologists, artists, writers, engineers, textile merchants, pharma magnates, arms dealers—and yes, bankers—but also municipalities, cities, cantons, and the federal government, have collected, curated, exhibited and sponsored art over the past 700 years. Here are just some of the private citizens or communities who made large collections possible.

1440–1591

The Amerbach family, Basel

Known for: the Amerbach-Kabinett collection, purchased by the city of Basel, which passed it on to the University of Basel in 1661 and became the foundation of the Kunstmuseum Basel.

15TH TO 18TH CENTURIES

Civic libraries like those in Zurich, Geneva and Bern

Known for: saving the collections of private individuals to exhibit to the public.

1890

Lydia Welti-Escher, Zurich

Known for: donating her entire fortune to the Swiss Confederation to create the Gottfried Keller Foundation, which supports the cultural heritage of Switzerland.

1885–1965

Oskar Reinhart, Winterthur

Known for: collecting European masterpieces that eventually filled two museums (see p.128).

1978 TO PRESENT

Léonard Gianadda, Martigny

Known for: creating the Fondation Pierre Gianadda, the home to three museums and a sculpture park (see p.90).

MARCO LUCCHETTI ART GALLERY

— *Where Batman meets Diabolik*

What at first looks like a simple comic book store at the bottom of the funicular from Lugano's train station expands to an upstairs gallery with works for sale by visual artists of the Ninth Art and Pop Art. The gallery holds around five exhibitions a year. A separate dedicated space also hosts readings and artworks inspired by comics, cartoons, *bande dessinées*, or animated films. Browse drawers full of original prints by legends like Hugo Pratt, Moebius and Enzo Facciolo, as well as contemporaries like Matteo Buffagni, Davide Zanella and Max Ross. The very friendly staff are always on hand for questions or impromptu discussions. Take a stroll through the old town after your visit; nearby restaurants offer pizza, pasta and polenta, with outdoor seating in the cobblestone piazzas.

VIA CATTEDRALE 3, 6900 LUGANO
MARCOLUCCHETTIARTGALLERY.CH

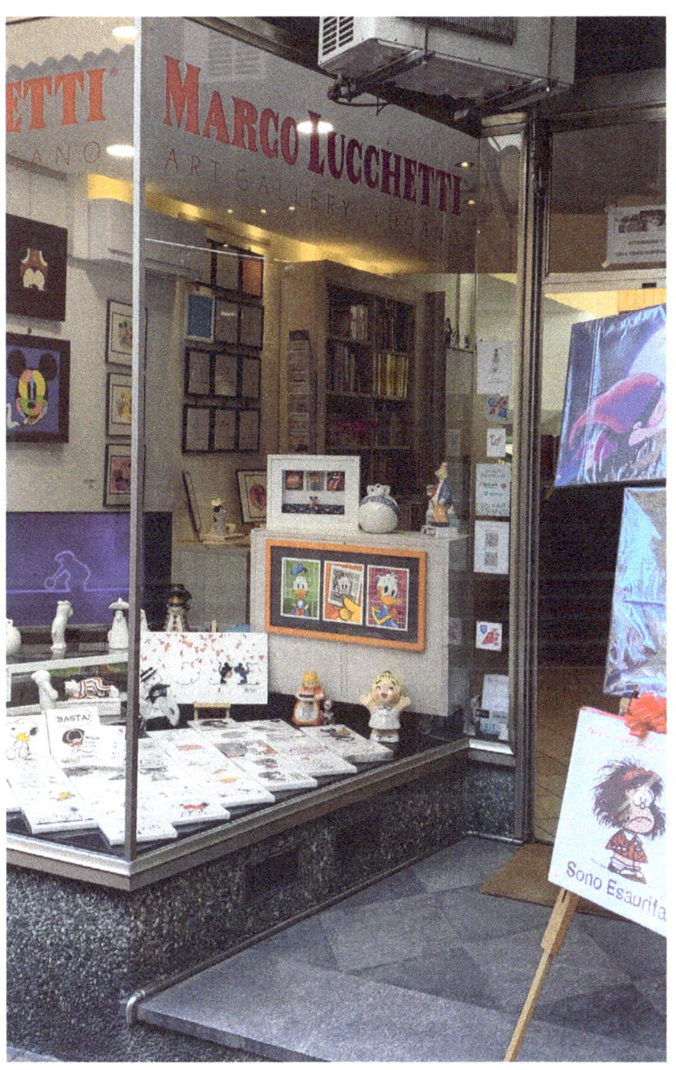
MARCO LUCCHETTI
BASTA!
Sono Esaurita

BALLY FOUNDATION VILLA HELENEUM

— *Emerging art in neoclassical luxury*

With two exhibitions per year, the Bally Foundation places a strong focus on upcoming artists who work in all media, with the villa's two floors wholly dedicated to each exhibition for five to six months. And what a villa it is! Built for a Parisian dancer in 1930, it has a long history as a cultural hotspot. Today, the blend of creative visionary talent, opulent building design and location makes it a perfect half-day destination for lovers of art, architecture and hiking. Walk or take the bus, as parking is rare and restricted. The villa, with its lush public garden and promenade, sits directly on Lake Lugano. The gorgeous *Sentiero dell'olivo* (Olive Trail) lakeside hiking path starts just down the street. The gallery's all-white café looks out over to Lugano's iconic Monte San Salvatore. You'll quickly start dreaming about moving in and collecting your own art.

VIA CORTIVO 24, 6976 LUGANO
BALLYFOUNDATION.CH

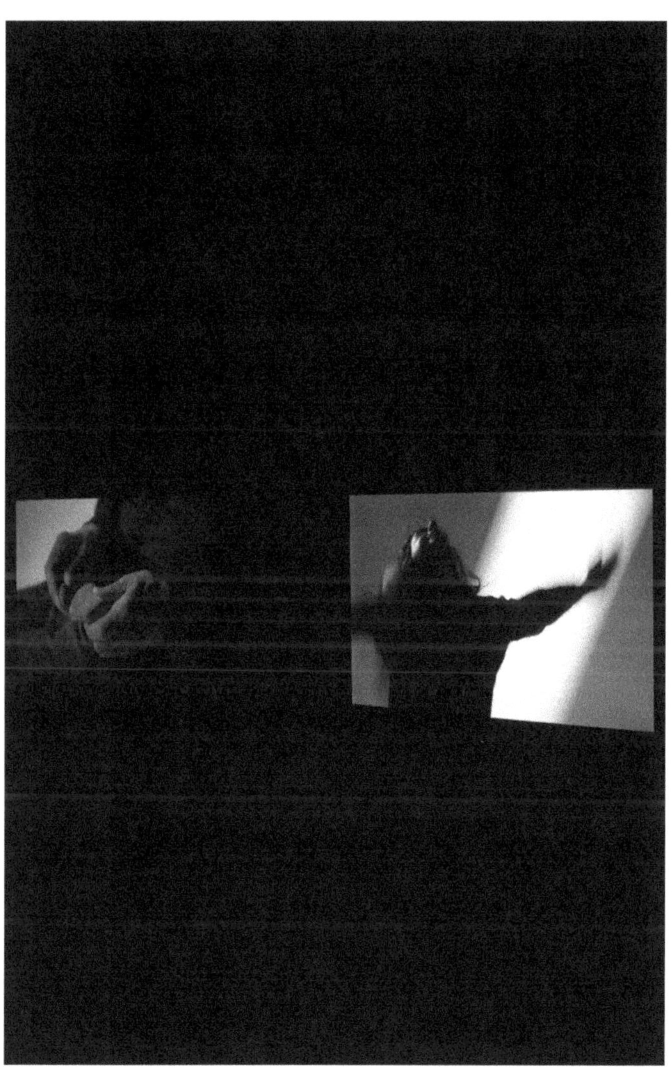

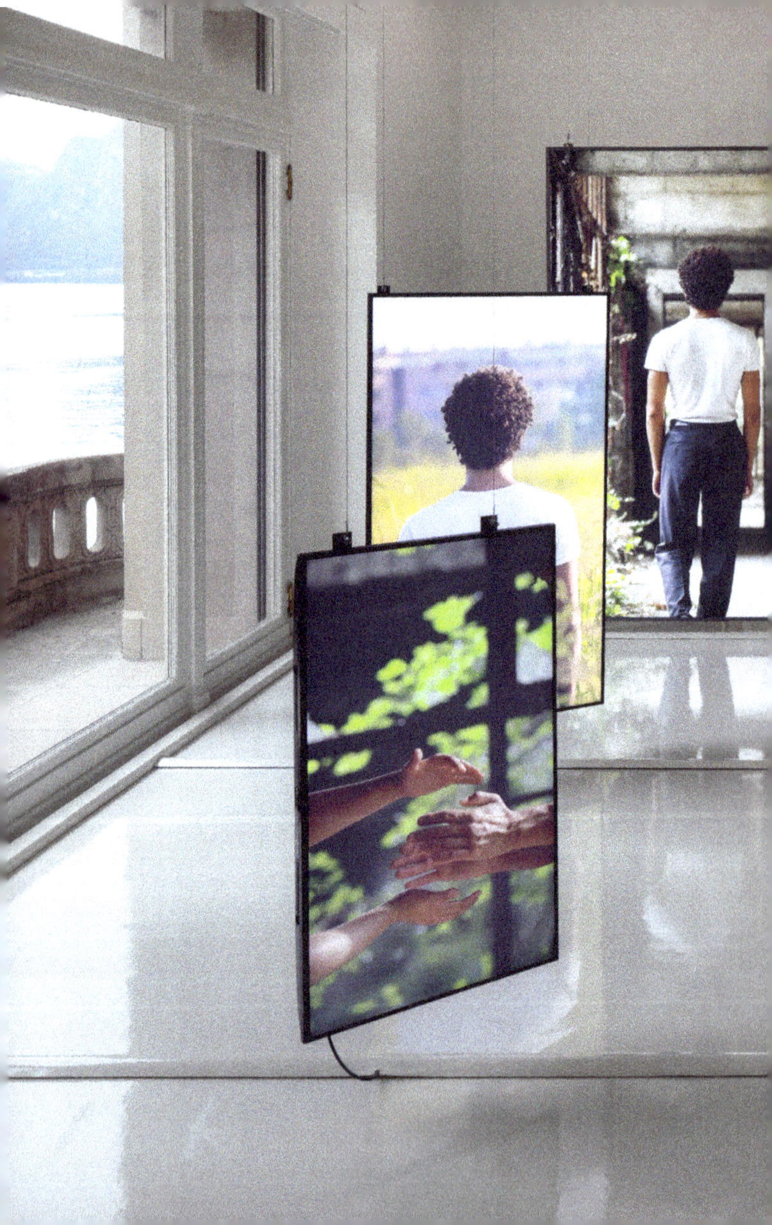

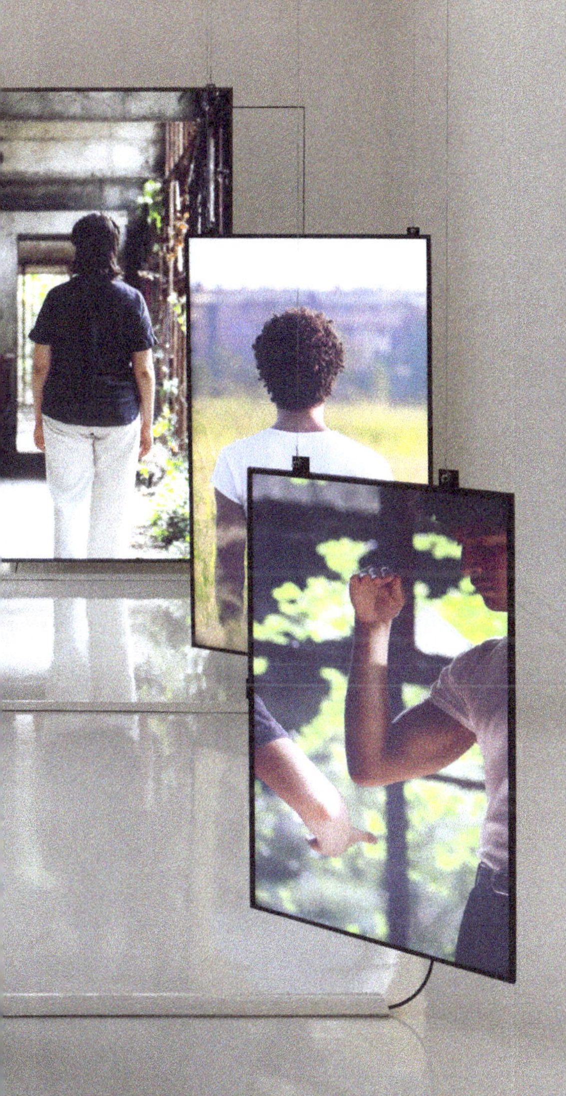

MASI LUGANO AND COLLEZIONE GIANCARLO E DANNA OLGIATI

— *Local heritage meets modern and contemporary*

With two sites—MASI LAC in Lugano's glass-and-steel lakeside cultural center and the 19th-century-renovated Palazzo Reali townhouse in the center of the old town—the MASI adds an espresso-on-the-piazza vacation vibe to your visit even if you're just there for a day. A collection strong on local artists (Filippo Franzoni, Cherubino Patà) blended with members of the international art scene with a connection to the area (Monica Bonvicini, Bertozzi & Casoni) is complemented by the Giancarlo and Danna Olgiati Collection of modern and contemporary art (Fortunato Depero, Carla Accardi) next door to MASI LAC. The latter holds only two three-month exhibitions a year. Stop for a glass of wine and whatever snack trend is whistling through the region (currently pinsa, bagels and poke bowls) on the spacious LAC square overlooking the lake.

MASI LAC, PIAZZA BERNARDINO LUINI 6 / PALAZZO REALI, VIA CANOVA 10, 6900 LUGANO
MASILUGANO.CH

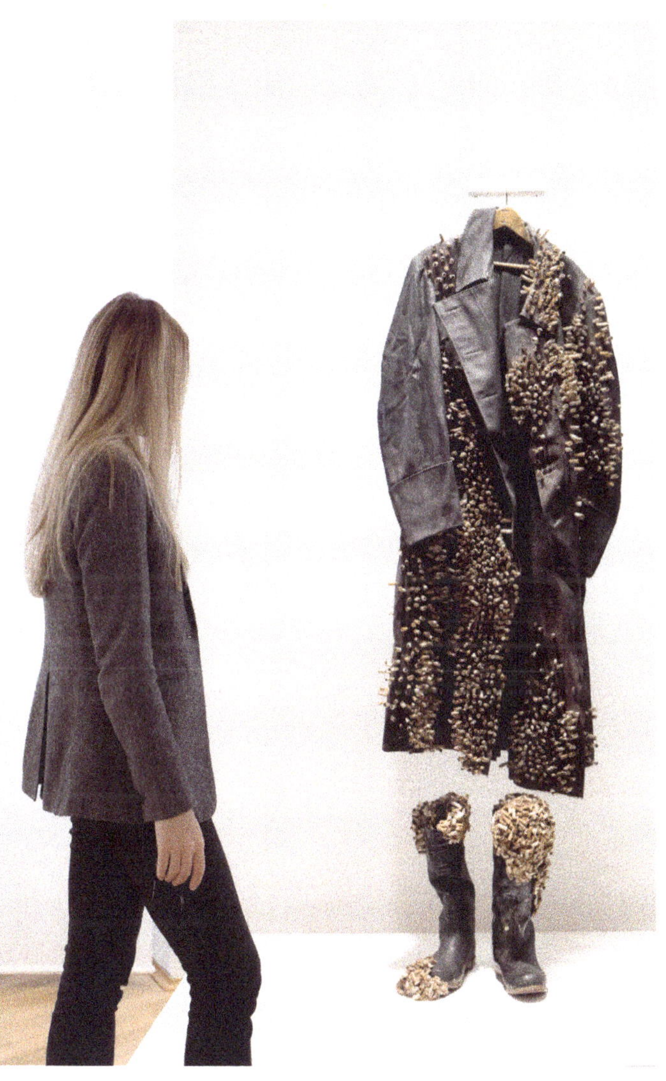

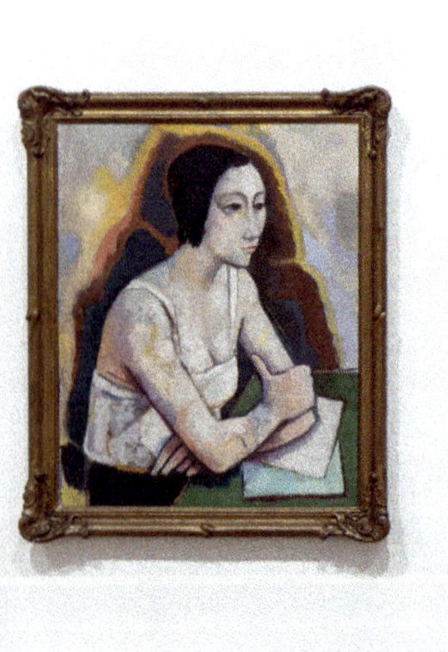

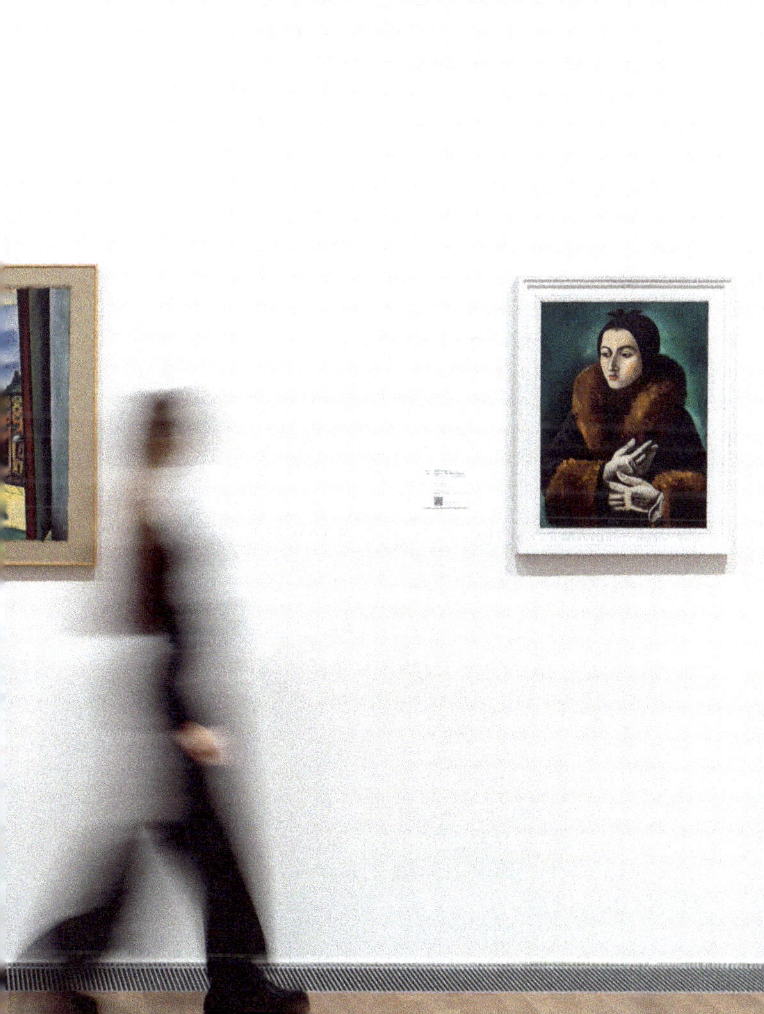

FONDATION PIERRE GIANADDA

— *Martigny's Roman heart*

This is a veritable medley of culture, conceived after the construction of a planned residential tower was halted by the discovery of a Roman temple on the site. The upper mezzanine of the two-tiered main building contains the Musée gallo-romain. Temporary art exhibits, which skew towards 19th- and 20th-century Europeans—such as Turner, Nadar and Dubuffet—are arranged around the temple's foundations on the ground floor. Amazingly, for such a relatively small venue, it also hosts world-class concerts featuring greats like Cecilia Bartoli and Martha Argerich. The site includes an antique car museum, a large park with approximately 50 sculptures by artists like Henry Moore and Niki de Saint Phalle, and two outbuildings for further temporary exhibitions: one with outdoor murals by French artist Sam Szafran. For the full effect, enjoy a local charcuterie plate on the self-serve cafeteria's outdoor patio overlooking the park.

RUE DU FORUM 59, 1920 MARTIGNY
GIANADDA.CH

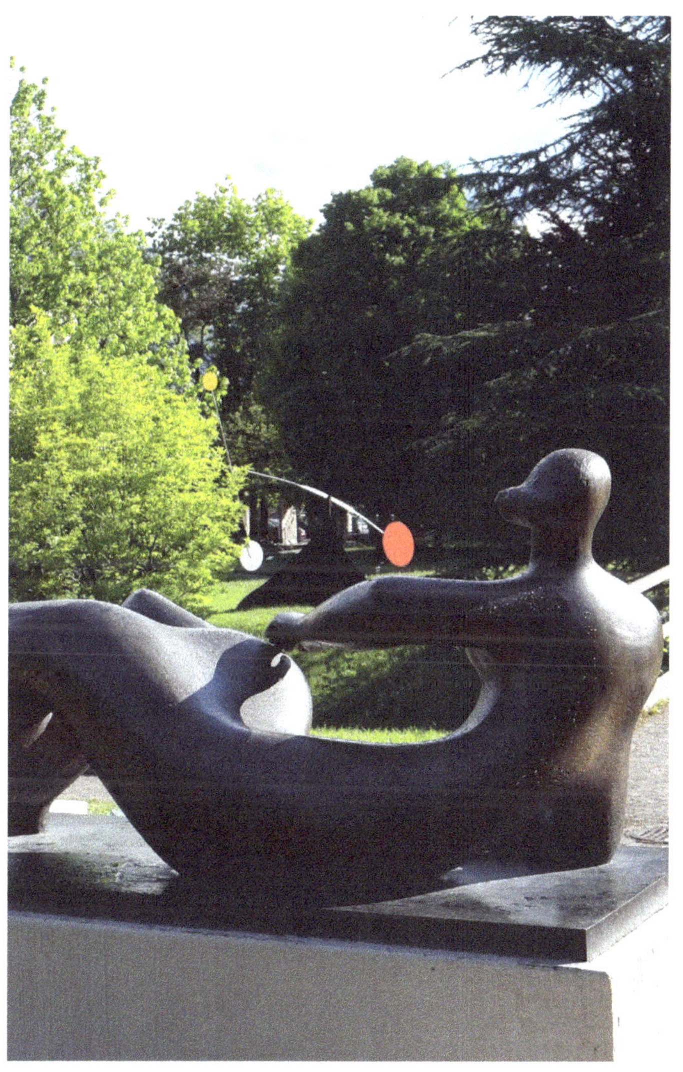

HR GIGER MUSEUM

— *A biomechanical world in medieval surrounds*

The fact that HR Giger's style belongs to the oxymoronic-sounding fantastic realism fits perfectly with the site of his private museum. Gruyères (yes, like the cheese) is the last place you'd expect to see his famous airbrushed images of aliens (yes, those) and erotic female biomechanisms. The medieval hilltop town is a symbol of all that is quintessentially Swiss (cheese and pocketknife shops, cows, Alps). In 1997, Giger purchased a small château there, turning it into an exhibition space that now often startles unsuspecting tourists who stumble upon it by chance. The museum is a collection of rooms linked together by steep stairs and narrow balconies, and does not offer wheelchair access. The bar is "a must" experience, but maybe don't get drunk there: with an amazing, vaulted ceiling designed to look like a row of vertebrae, it feels like you're (already) inside the alien's stomach.

RUE DU CHÂTEAU 2, 1663 GRUYÈRES
HRGIGERMUSEUM.COM

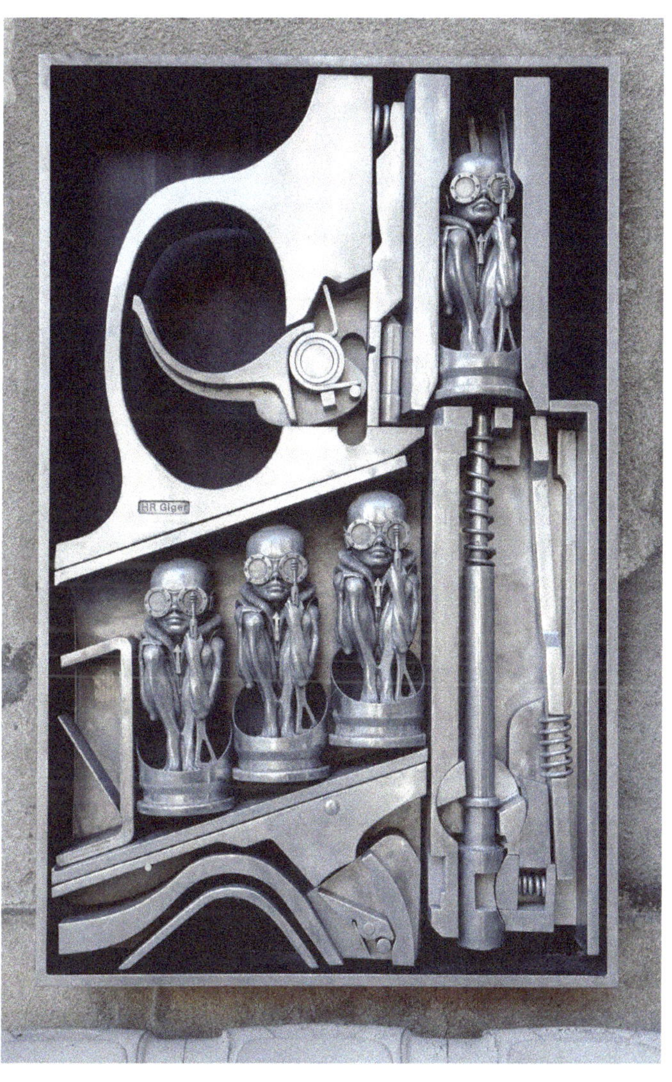
HR Giger

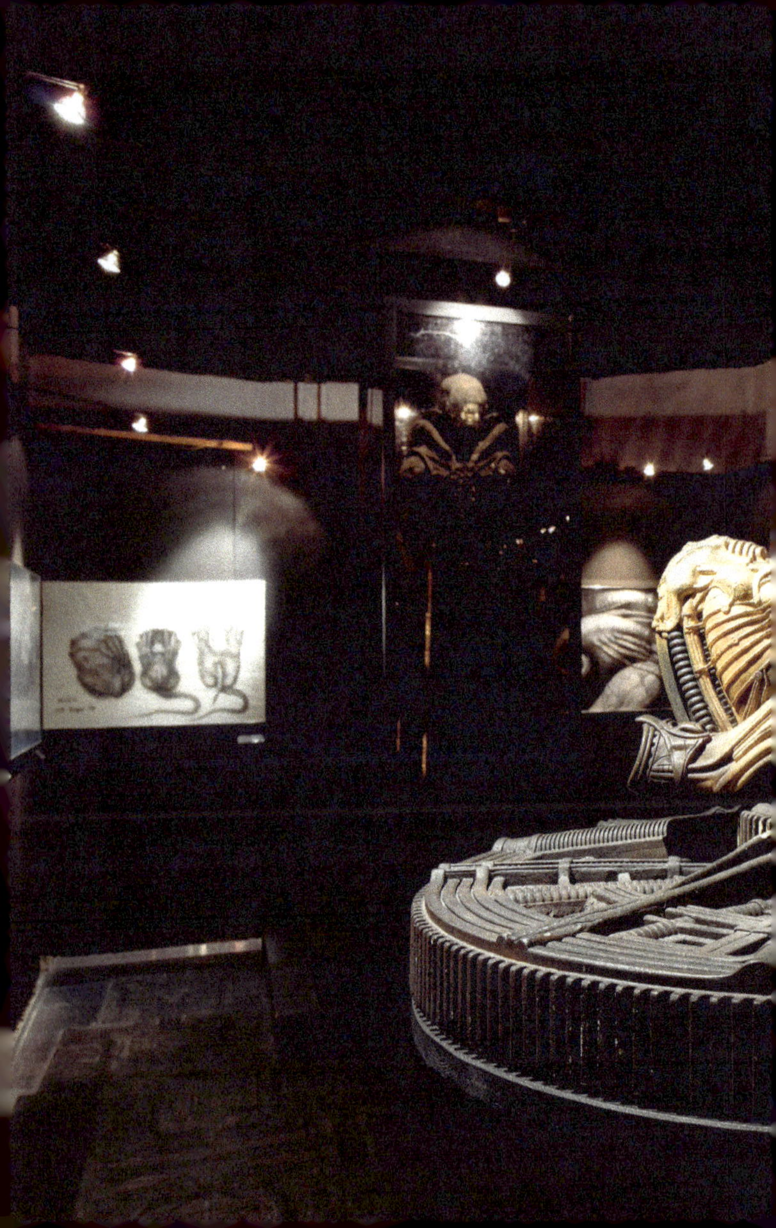

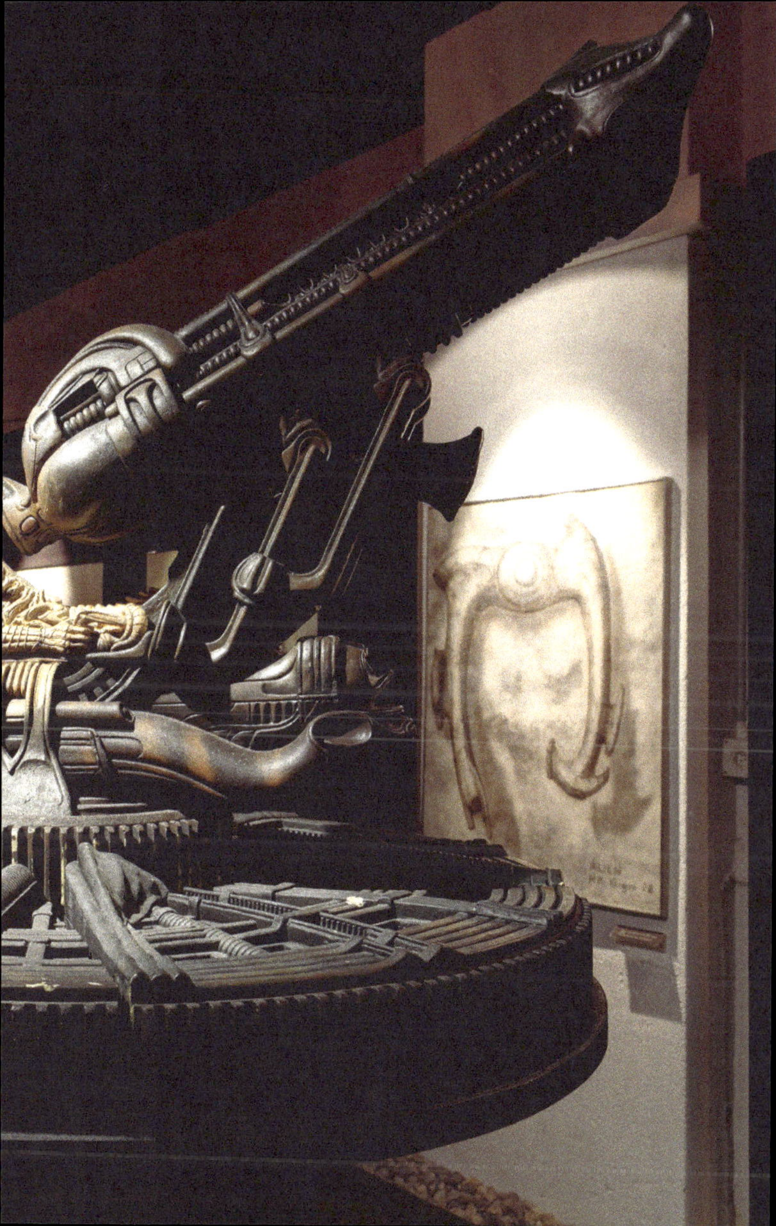

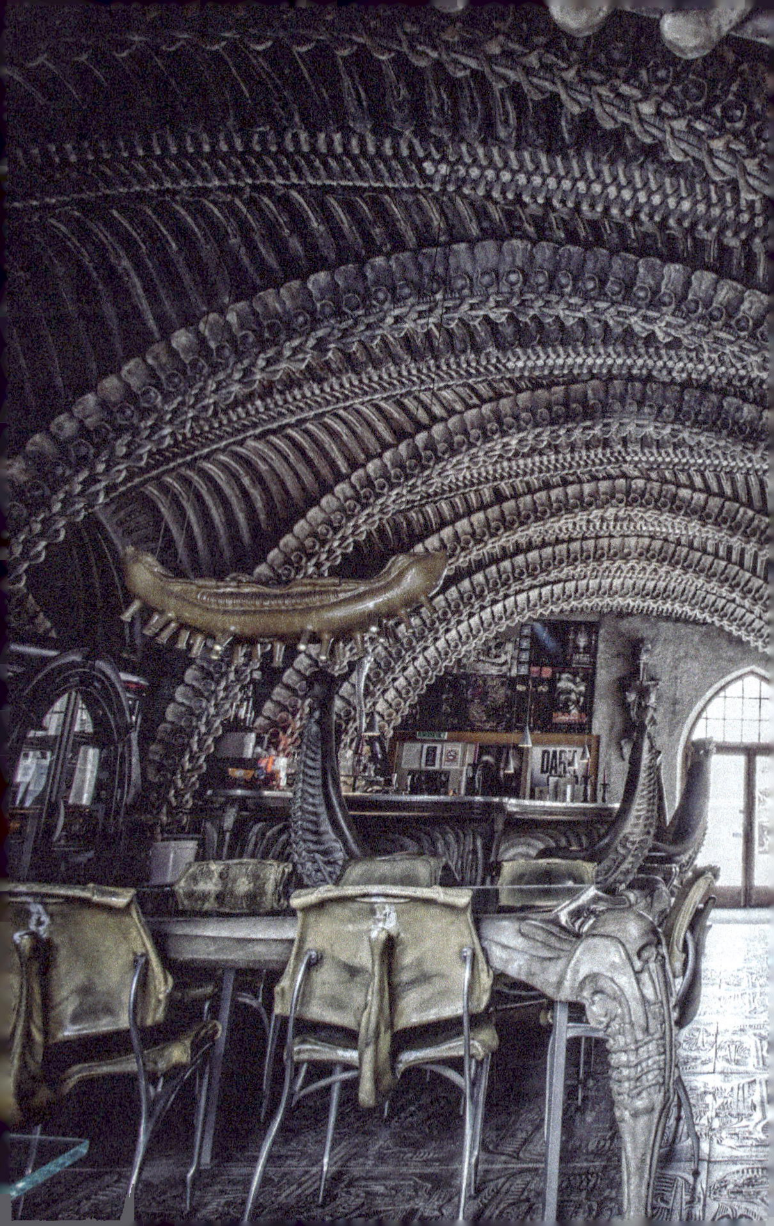

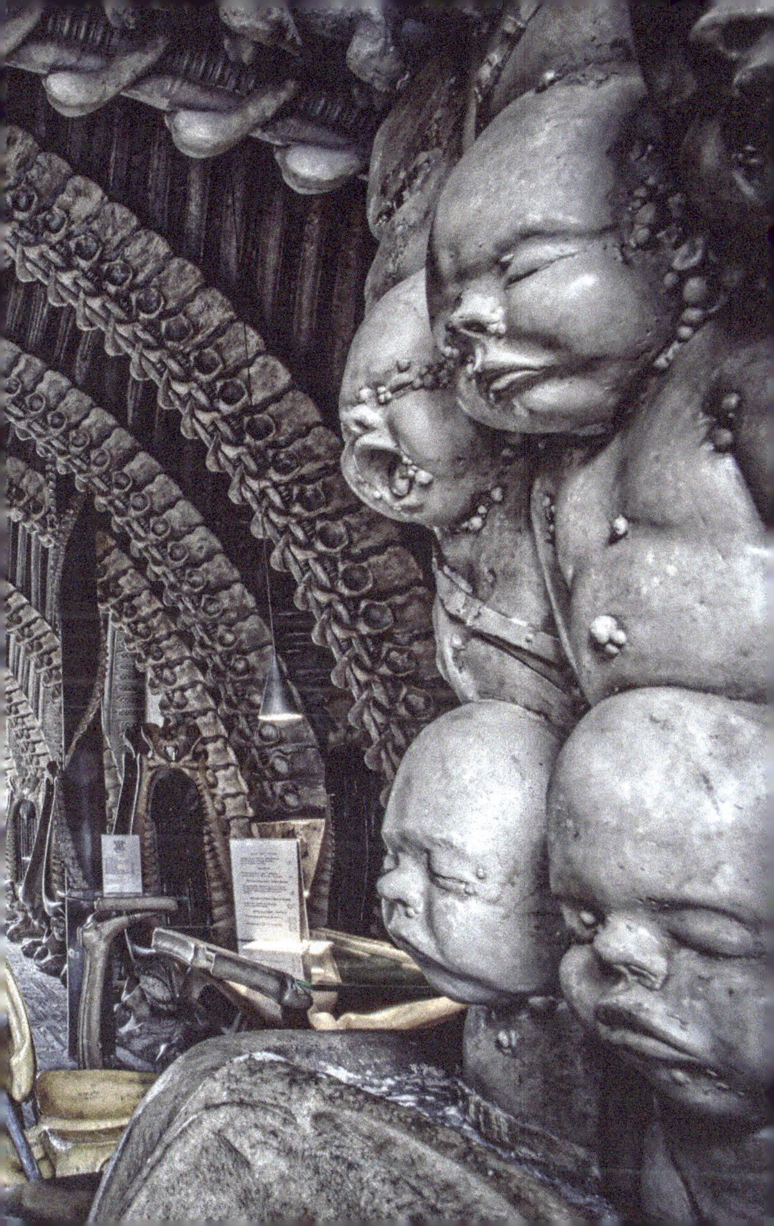

COLLECTION DE L'ART BRUT

— Art that reflects pure personal truths

"Art Brut" (raw art) was defined by French painter Jean Dubuffet as works created by self-taught, non-conformist artists. His collection is based on 133 pieces from individuals like Giovanni Abrignani and Bogosav Živković: prisoners, inmates of psychiatric clinics or otherwise solitary artists, uninterested in movements, who instead listened to their inner voice. Their works are exhibited in the 18th-century Château de Beaulieu: one of its more intriguing "X-slept-here" guests was Jacques Necker, Louis XVI's finance minister, who nudged the French Revolution along by informing the people of Their Majesty's spendthrift ways. While the outside still reflects its fancy castle past, the interior is repurposed, to stunning effect, in modern black and white. Its program for kids is adorably called "mini-Brut." The adjacent Auberge de Beaulieu bar and restaurant serves a mix of US and EU hits.

11, AV. DES BERGIÈRES, 1004 LAUSANNE
ARTBRUT.CH

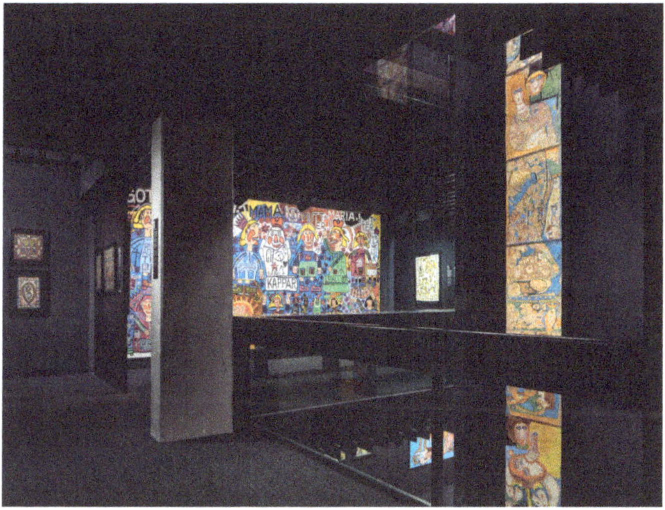

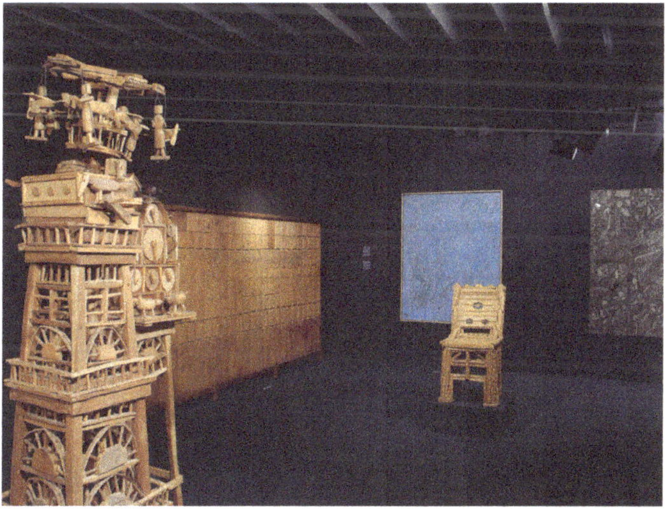

PLATEFORME 10: MCBA, MUDAC AND PHOTO ELYSÉE

— *Lausanne's one-stop art destination*

Plateforme 10 is home to the three cantonal art museums of Vaud. MCBA is the classic art gallery, with large 18th-to-20th-century collections of Swiss artists, such as Louis Ducros and Félix Vallotton. If you want to see a large, gilt-framed painting of a cow on an Alp, this is your spot. But it's not stuck in the past, also housing abstract and new media pieces. Mudac's focus is on design with a broad, energetic lens that is not afraid to look at social issues. Photo Elysée's photography exhibitions trace the medium from its beginnings to today's digital world. It's also home to Charlie Chaplin's entire photo archive. Plateforme 10 is a meeting point for art lovers, with an esplanade flanked by smaller exhibition spaces, restaurants and bars to hang out in, plus the requisite gift shops to buy really cool stuff you don't actually need, but love on sight.

AVENUE LOUIS-RUCHONNET 1, 1003 LAUSANNE
PLATEFORME10.CH

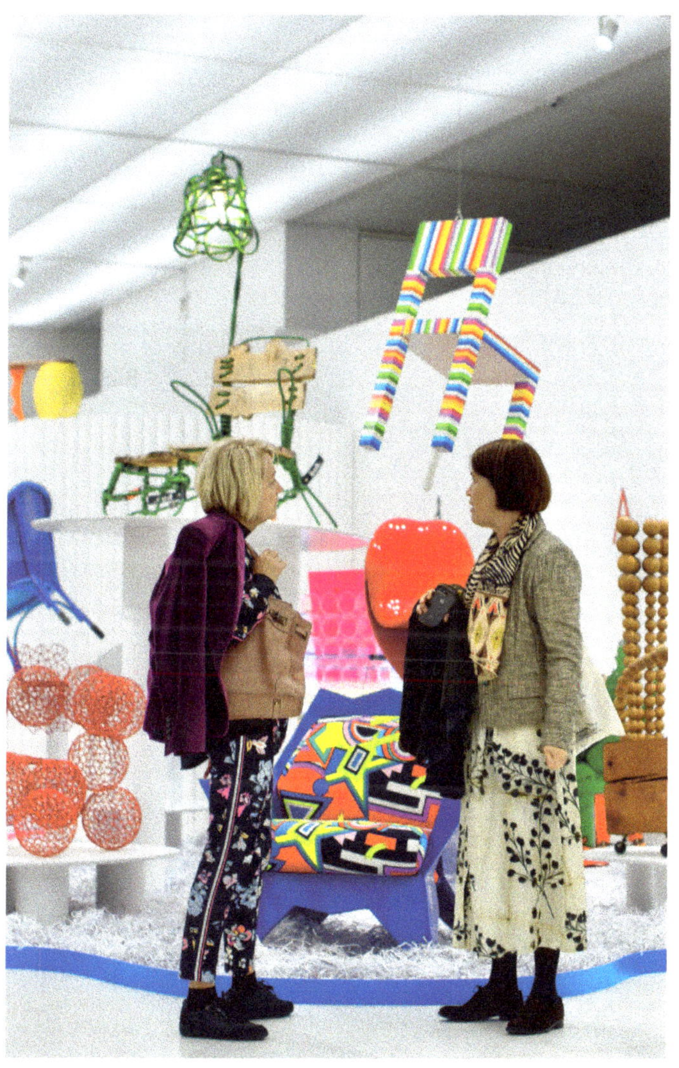

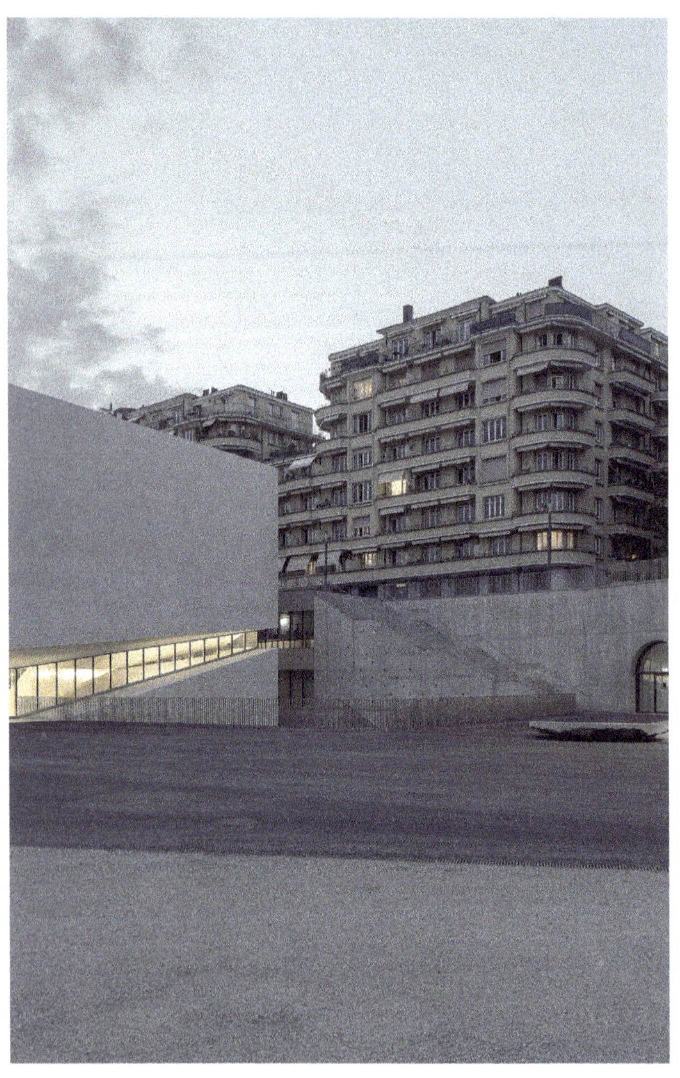

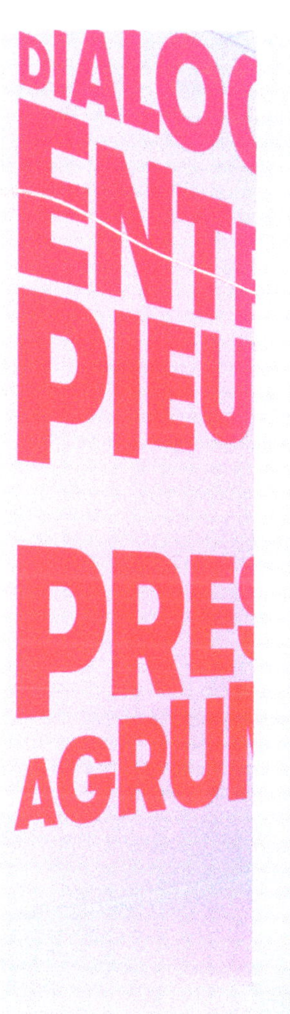

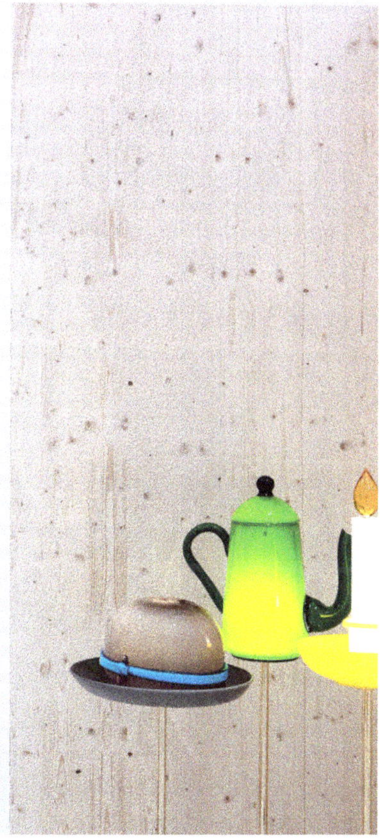

FONDATION DE L'HERMITAGE

— *Remarkable collections in the heart of Lausanne*

Another in a significant number of Switzerland's former patrician villas turned art museums, the Fondation de l'Hermitage focuses on 19th- and 20th-century paintings. Its renowned *Fondation pour l'Art et la Culture* collection of 800 donated works is augmented by exhibitions using temporary loans from other institutions, as well as holding concerts, workshops and other outreach activities. In-house acquisitions include paintings by local artists such as René Auberjonois, Jean Lecoultre and Gérard de Palézieux, as well as an exceptional collection of Chinese porcelain. It pays to go on a sunny day for the full effect of the villa's gorgeous surrounding hilltop park, with views over Lake Geneva. A highlight of the museum's events is a guided private tour complemented by a gourmet dinner hosted by the on-site restaurant L'esquisse.

ROUTE DU SIGNAL 2, 1018 LAUSANNE
FONDATION-HERMITAGE.CH

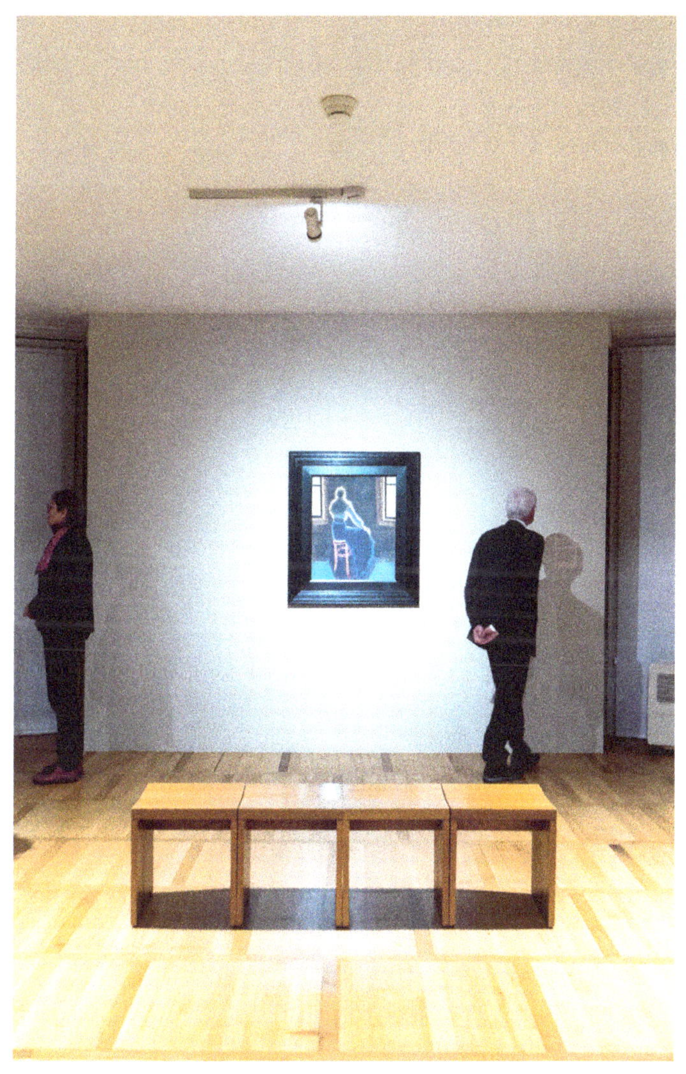

CHÂTEAU DE PRANGINS

— *The Age of Enlightenment meets the present*

The Prangins Swiss National Museum is housed in an 18th-century castle. Its vision of "Swiss heritage as art" gives master crafts such as woodwork, ceramics and textiles just as much importance as the beaux arts. Its eight permanent collections of historical objects (chintz, detail-laden baroque interiors, a portrait gallery—yes, that's Voltaire) are balanced out by contemporary exhibitions, like annual Swiss Press Photo Award winners (Alex Kühni, Karine Bauzin). The grounds include a huge, historical kitchen garden that makes for a gorgeous stroll and produces over 200 varieties of fruits, vegetables and herbs. The path lures you back to Le Café du Château, which turns the garden's seasonal harvests into fabulous lunches. There is outdoor seating on the castle terrace and staff can make a picnic basket for you to take to your favorite corner of the five-hectare estate.

AVENUE GÉNÉRAL GUIGUER 3, 1197 PRANGINS
CHATEAUDEPRANGINS.CH

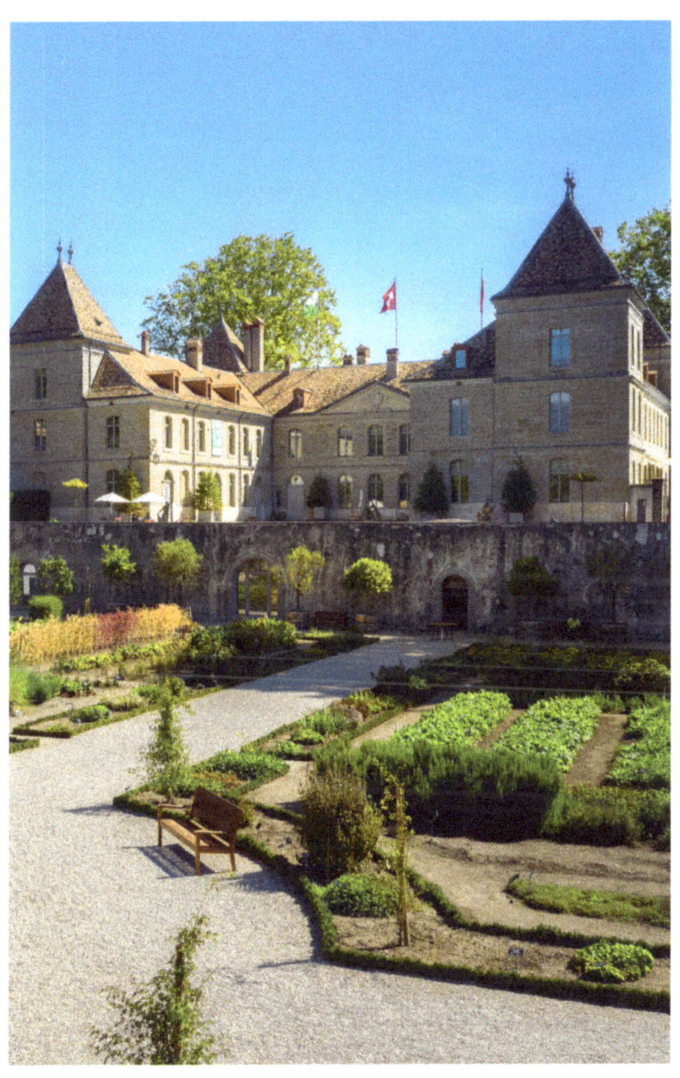

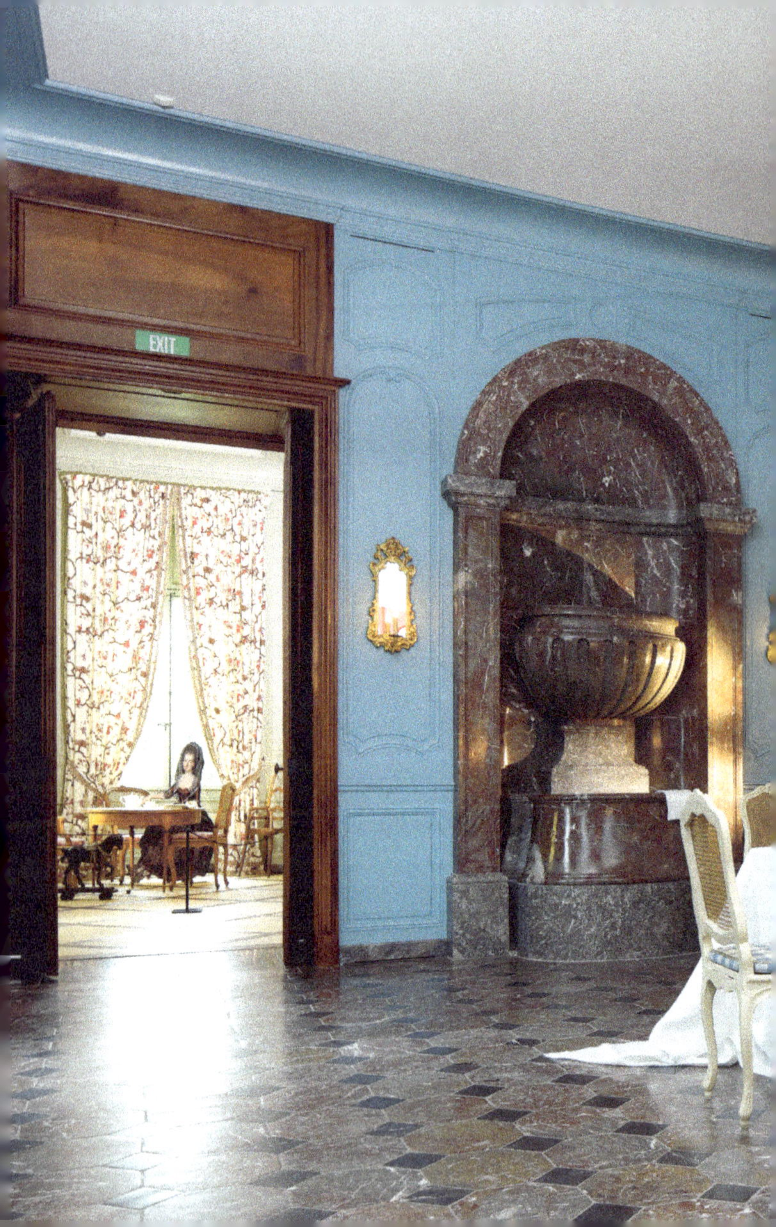
EXIT

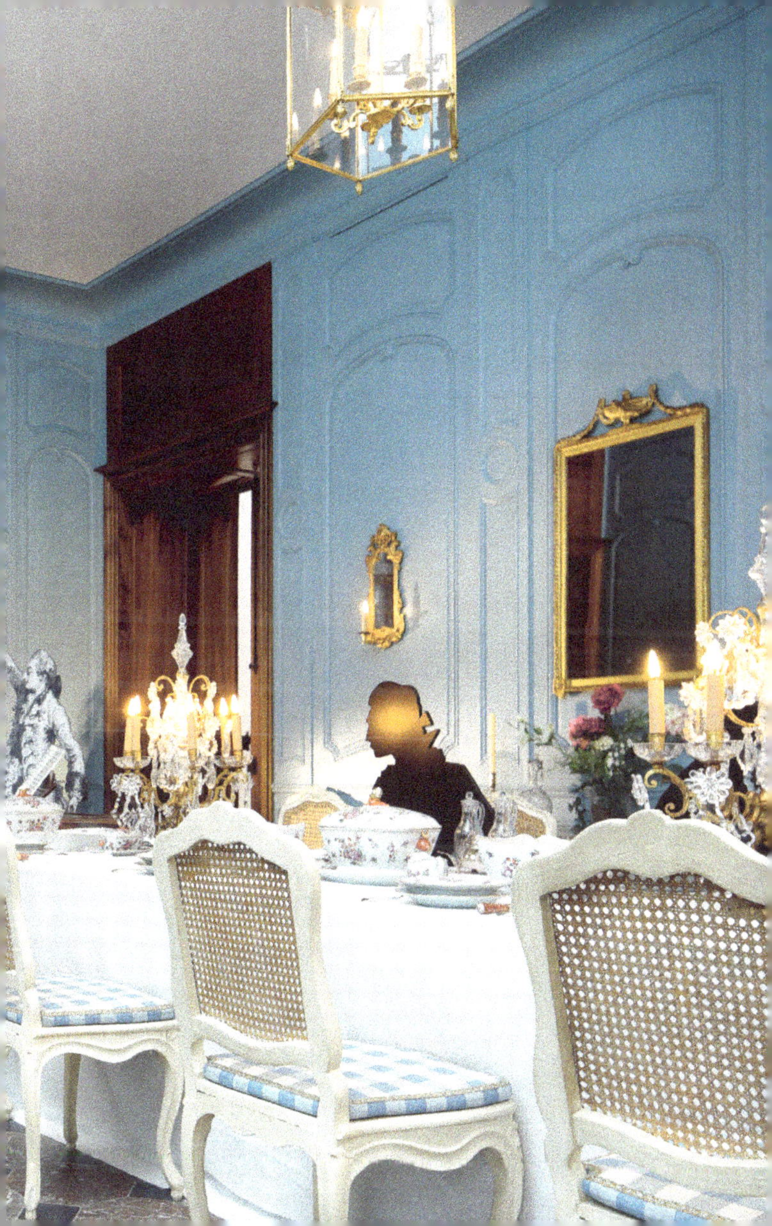

BUGS THAT EAT ART

If you think the biggest threat to art collections is burglars, you're wrong—it's insects who munch their way through wood, paper or textiles. They can ruin a 2000-year-old irreplaceable piece of culture in a matter of weeks. Here are some of the biggest culprits and what they love most:

WOOD

Statues, furniture and frames

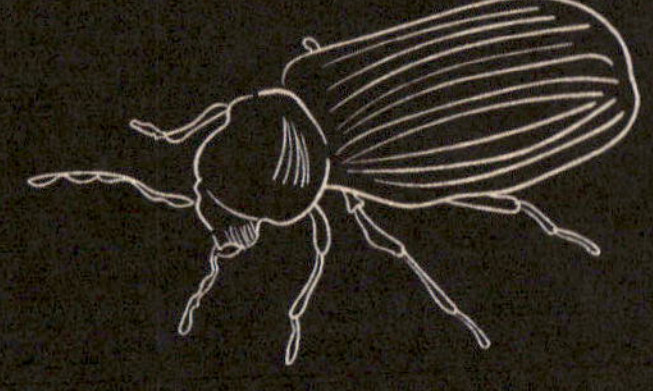

- **Anobium punctatum**
  The common furniture beetle
- **Xestobium rufovillosum**
  Death watch beetle

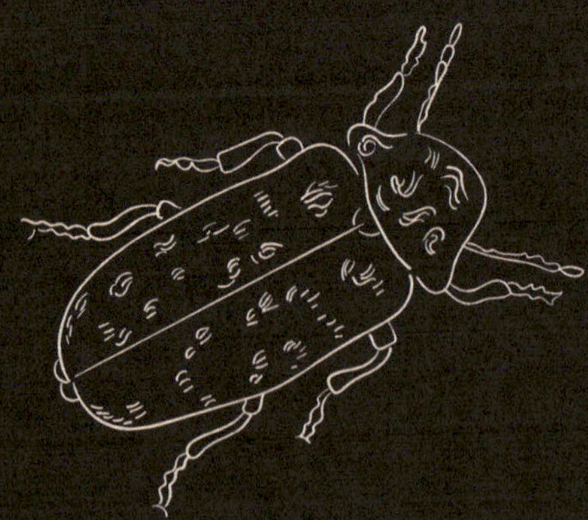

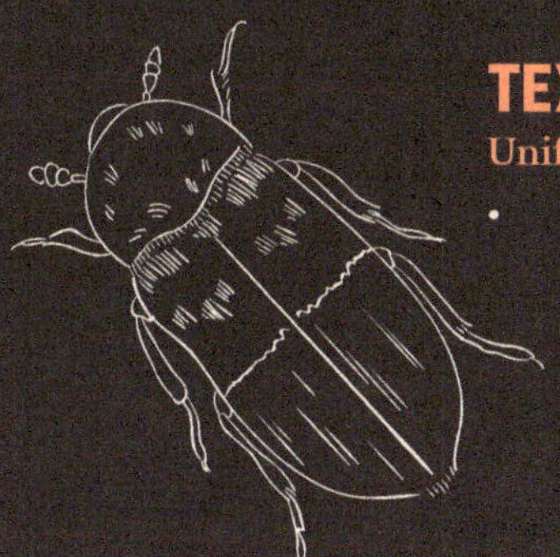

TEXTILES & PROTEINS

Uniforms, hats and lace

- **Dermestes lardarius**
  The larder beetle

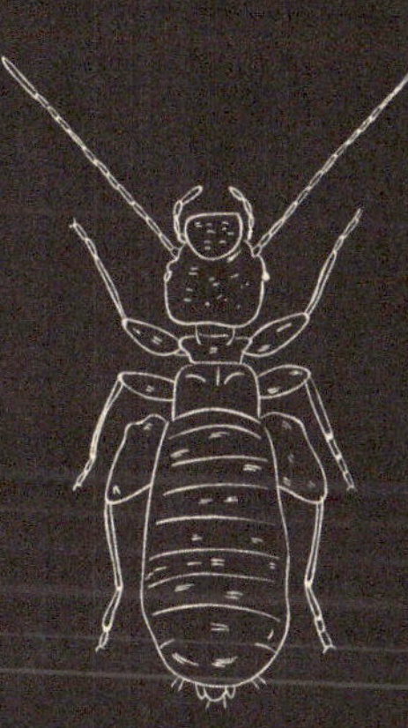

BINDING PASTE

Books

- **Liposcelis species**
  The book louse or psocodea

PAPER

Books, manuscripts and maps

- **Ctenolepisma longicaudatum**
  The long-tailed silverfish

SCHWEIZERISCHES NATIONALMUSEUM SAMMLUNGSZENTRUM

— *The national museum's central archives*

The federal government's Swiss National Museum has three locations—the Landesmuseum Zurich, the Château de Prangins and the Forum Schweizer Geschichte Schwyz—with a mission to present the history of Swiss culture. Boasting a collection of some 870,000 objects that grows constantly, the museum has central archives where new donations are accepted and old things are restored and, as much as possible, protected from destruction by insects, mold and mice. The museum contains everything from paintings and religious iconography to photographs and boxes of COVID-19 vaccines. A recent visit revealed a storage unit lined with ten Christs on the cross at one end and Credit Suisse signage at the other. The archives are not generally open to the public, but themed tours are available once a month in German, French and English—be sure to book two weeks in advance.

LINDENMOOSSTRASSE 1, 8910 AFFOLTERN AM ALBIS
SAMMLUNGSZENTRUM.CH

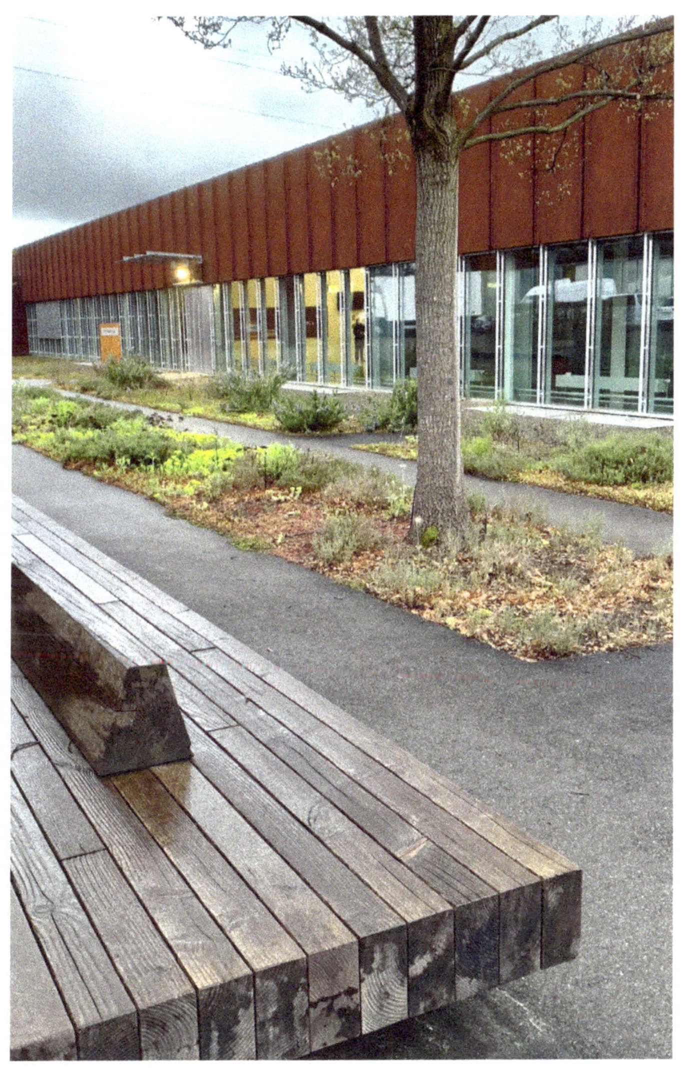

BRUNO WEBER PARK

— *A fairytale of fantastic realism*

In 1962, before Niki de Saint Phalle had even thought of making her Tarot Garden in Tuscany, the outstanding Swiss artist Bruno Weber began creating sculptures out of concrete, iron and glass on his family's property above the small town of Dietikon. Assisted by his wife, Maria Anna, and his daughters over a period of more than 40 years, he built a magical, 15,000 m² world of creatures, features and fantastic buildings—think Antoni Gaudí on a mind-altering trip to Thailand. The paths in this extraordinary, family-friendly park are lined with enormous beasts that are not quite giraffes or snakes, wind through archways that look like they would eat you, and take you to fanciful pavilions and ponds, with more otherworldly surprises around every corner. A gorgeous kiosk offers snacks and drinks. Check the website when planning your visit: it's not open every day.

ZUR WEINREBE 3, 8953 DIETIKON
WEBERPARK.CH

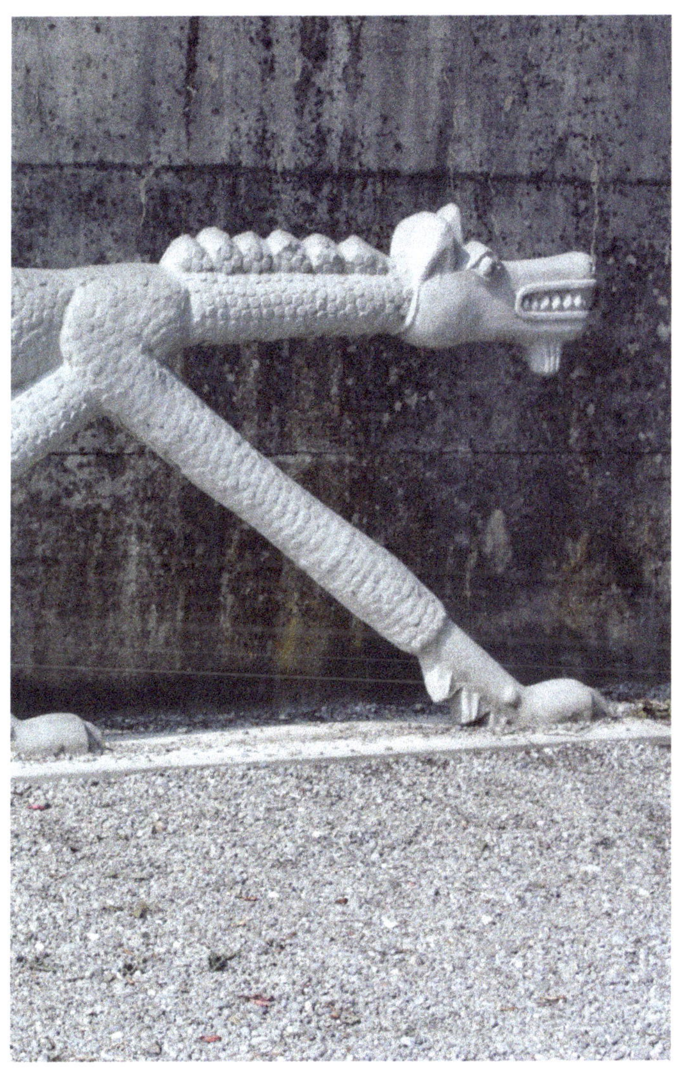

GALERIE BRUNO BISCHOFBERGER

— *A private gallery behind intricate ribbons of concrete*

When legendary art dealer Bruno Bischofberger—the man who brought international Pop Art to Switzerland—moved his gallery from downtown Zurich to the top of the hill in Männedorf, he made sure there would be a reason to come all that way. In addition to the greats he represents—from Andy Warhol and Miquel Barceló to David Salle and Dokoupil—the building designed by his daughter Nina Baier-Bischofberger and her husband Florian Baier is in itself worth the visit. Tucked into a residential neighborhood, its walls alternate between a myriad of "suction cups" and waves of concrete over glass; *Architectural Digest* calls it a masterpiece. Inside, Bischofberger collections also include European folk art, prehistoric stone art, and glass and ceramic design. Check opening times before you go, as they are irregular, and there is no official street parking.

WEISSENRAINSTRASSE 1, 8708 MÄNNEDORF
BRUNOBISCHOFBERGER.COM

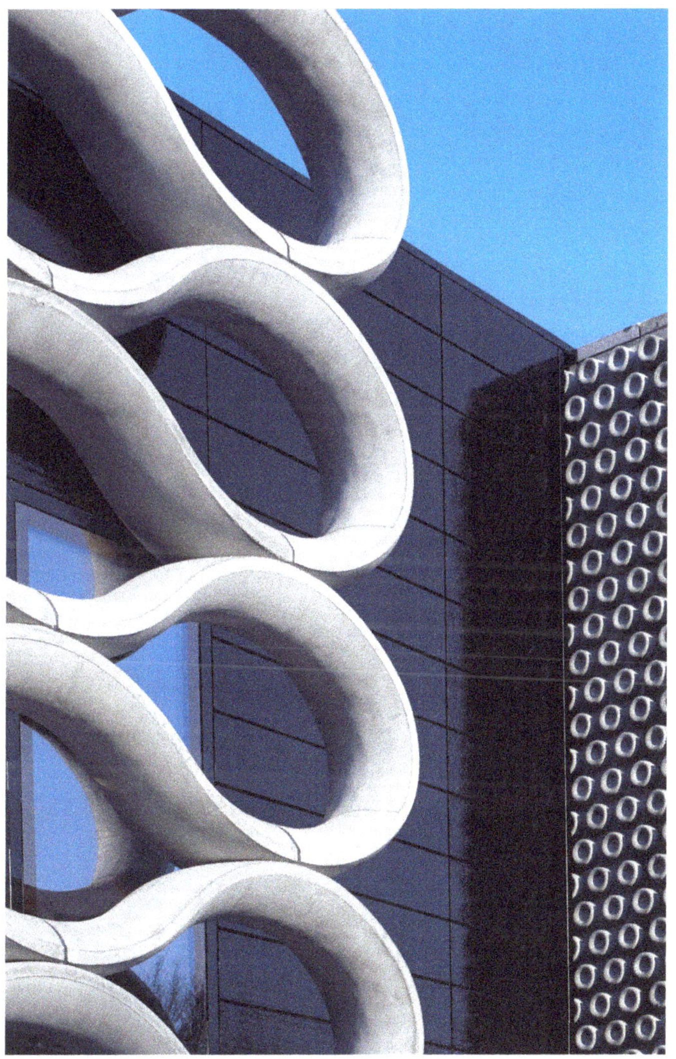

FOTOMUSEUM WINTERTHUR

— *Switzerland's leading photography museum*

The focus here is on photography—documentary, narrative, conceptual, fine art, post—and all its offshoots. Housed within the modernized interiors of brick industrial buildings that date back to 1877, the themed exhibitions and special shows of contemporary photographers, such as Poulomi Basu and Ester Vonplon, attract visitors from all over the world. A past highlight was an exhibition curated by Tilda Swinton. Thanks to talks with artists, workshops and other outreach programs, the museum presents all facets of photography to the public. The site also includes the Center for Photography, which is run jointly by Fotomuseum Winterthur and Fotostiftung Schweiz. The center houses a research library, museum shop, bistro, archives, exhibition space, and a public library with approximately 30,000 books and publications.

GRÜZENSTRASSE 44 + 45, 8400 WINTERTHUR
FOTOMUSEUM.CH

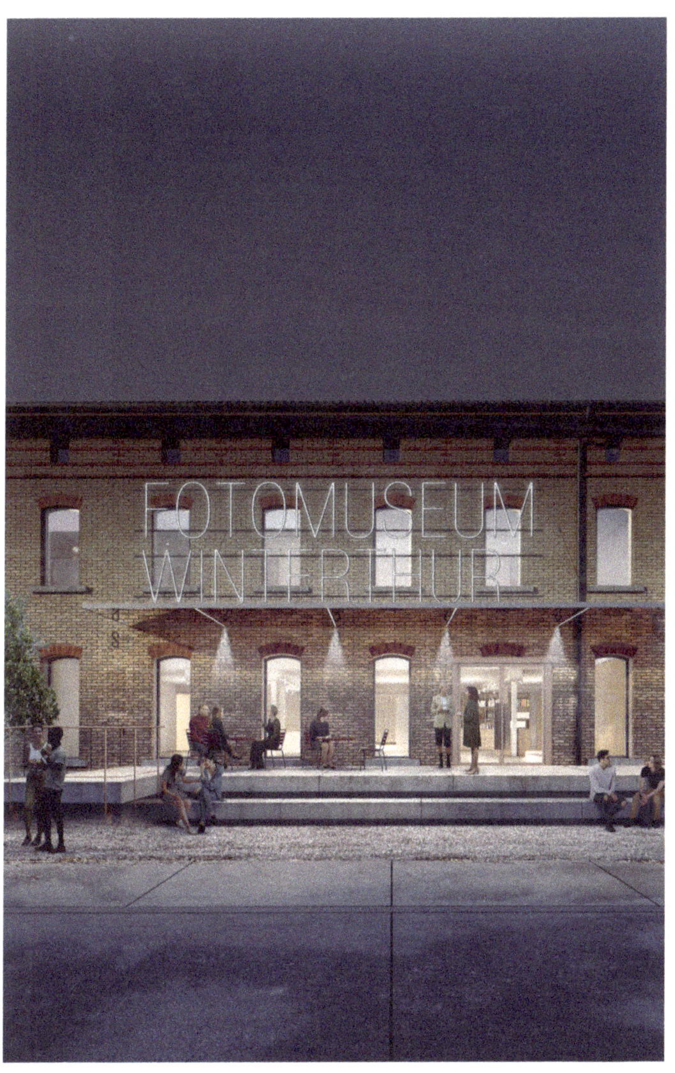
FOTOMUSEUM
WINTERTHUR

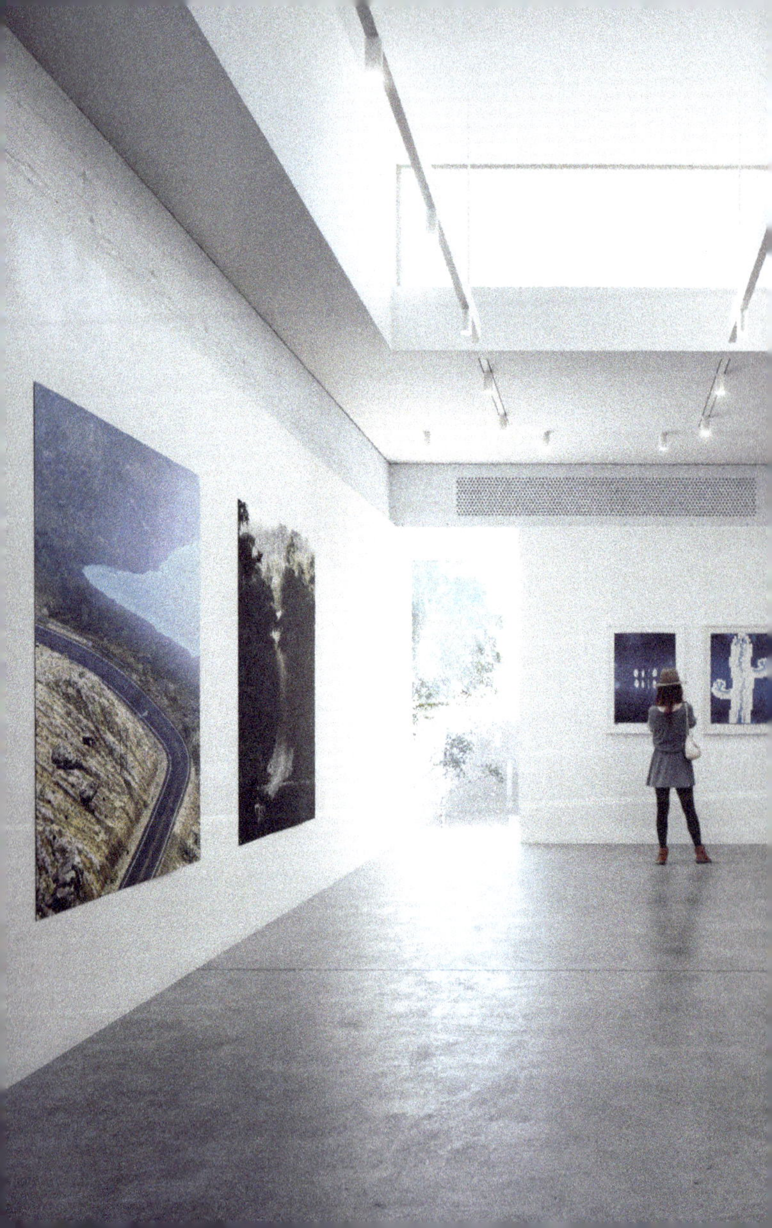

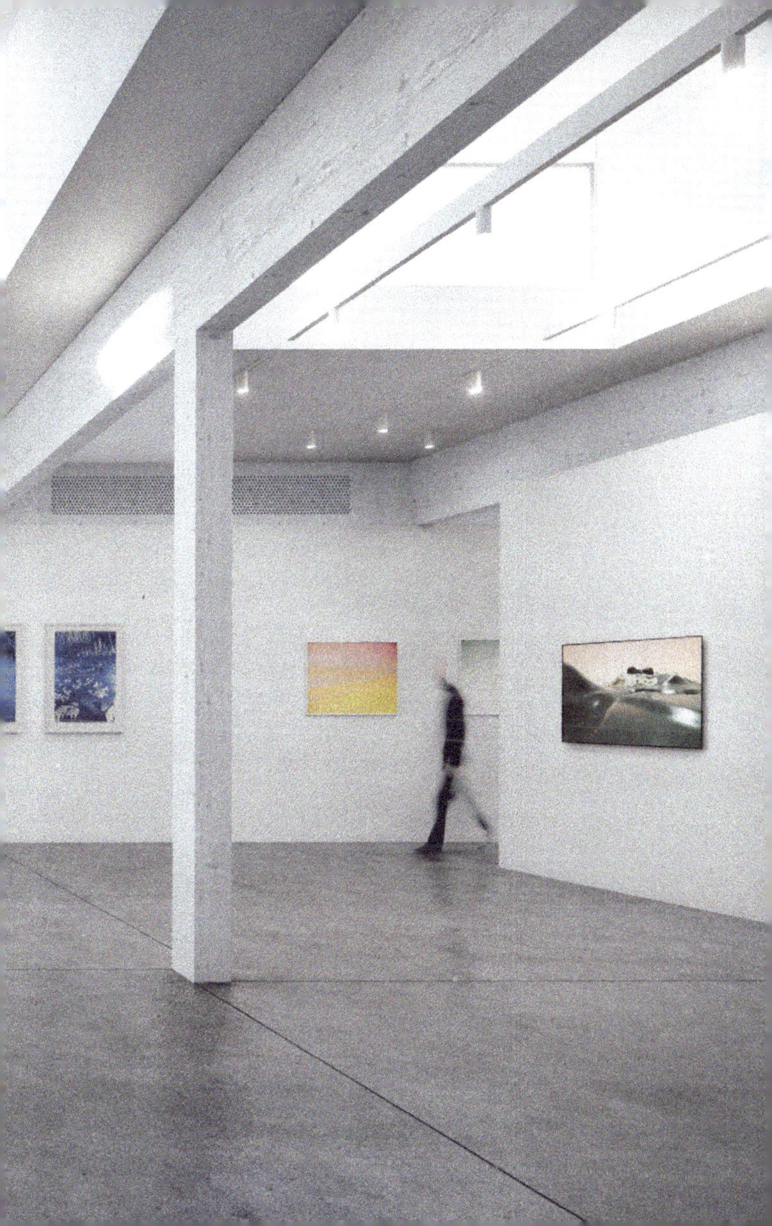

KUNST MUSEUM WINTERTHUR

— *An extensive collection founded on a century of patronage*

The former industrial town of Winterthur owes its many art museums to the families that made their fortunes in textiles, machinery or imported goods. With the generated wealth, some acquired large art collections—many of which were donated to this museum over the past 100 years—including masterpieces by Monet, Bonnard and Maillol. The museum has continuously added contemporary works (Gerhard Richter, Pia Fries) and now boasts the fourth-largest public collection in Switzerland, after Basel, Bern and Zurich. Exhibitions highlight artists such as Silvia Bächli and Monica Bonvicini. The main Beim Stadthaus building is complemented by the Reinhart am Stadtgarten and the lush Villa Flora; your ticket gets you into all three. Winterthur has a veritable plethora of international food options around town.

MUSEUMSTRASSE 52, 8400 WINTERTHUR
KMW.CH

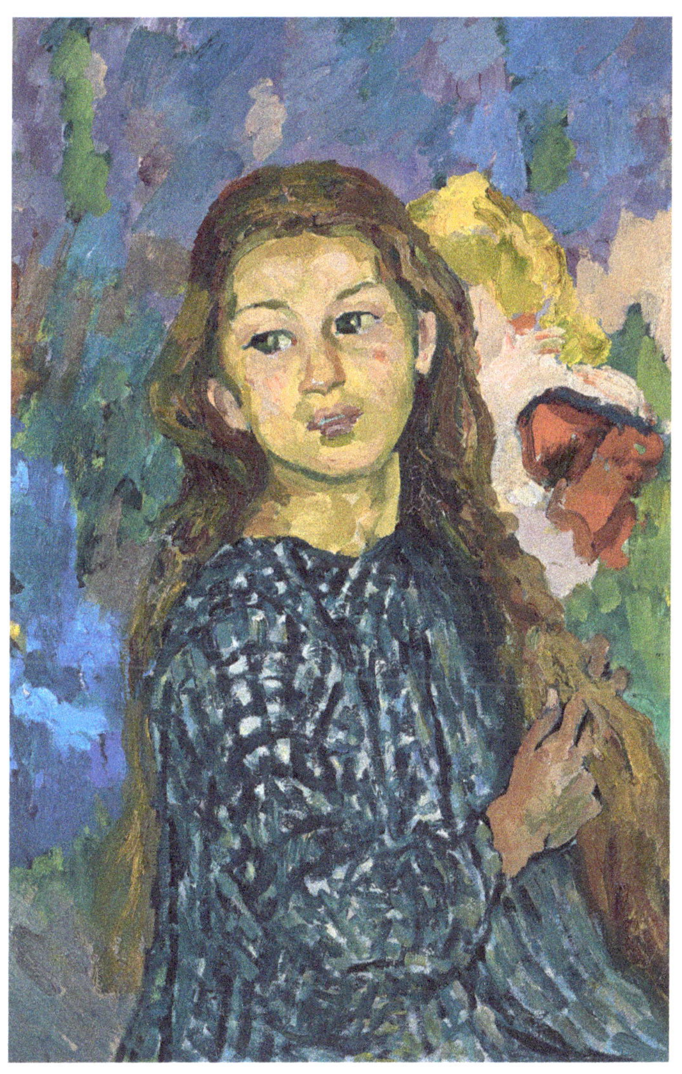

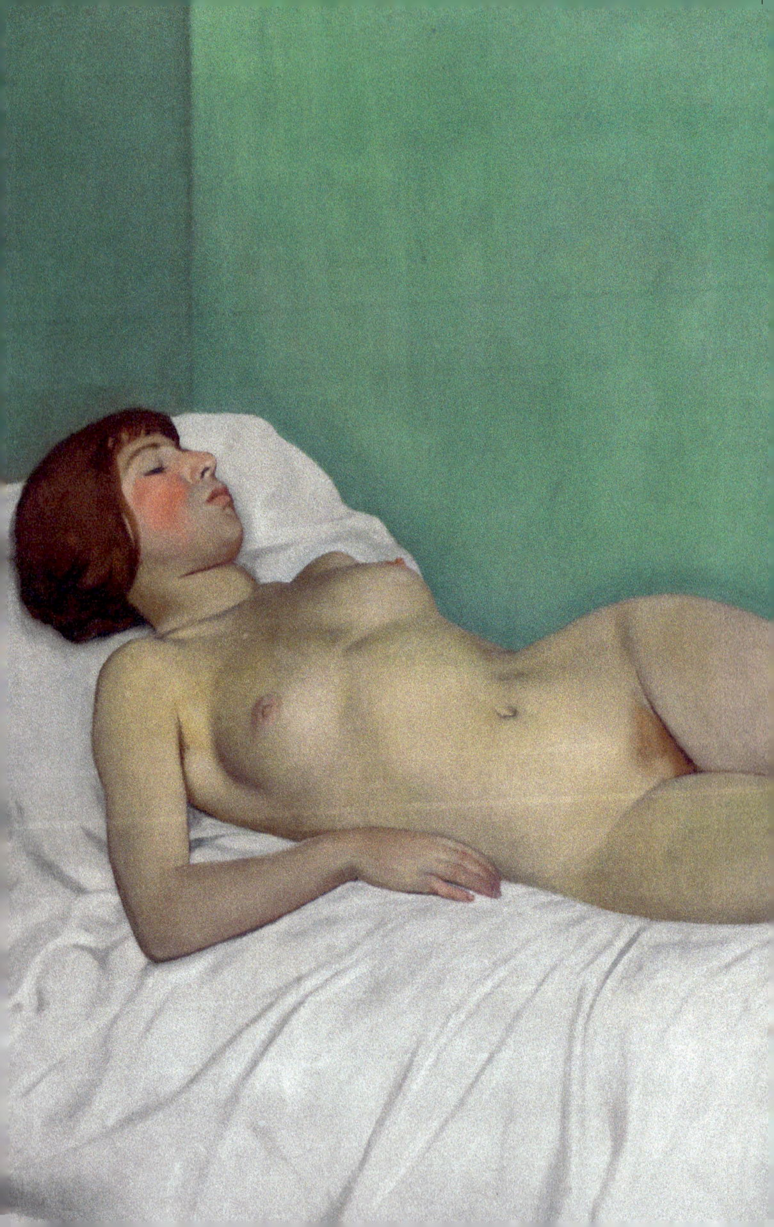

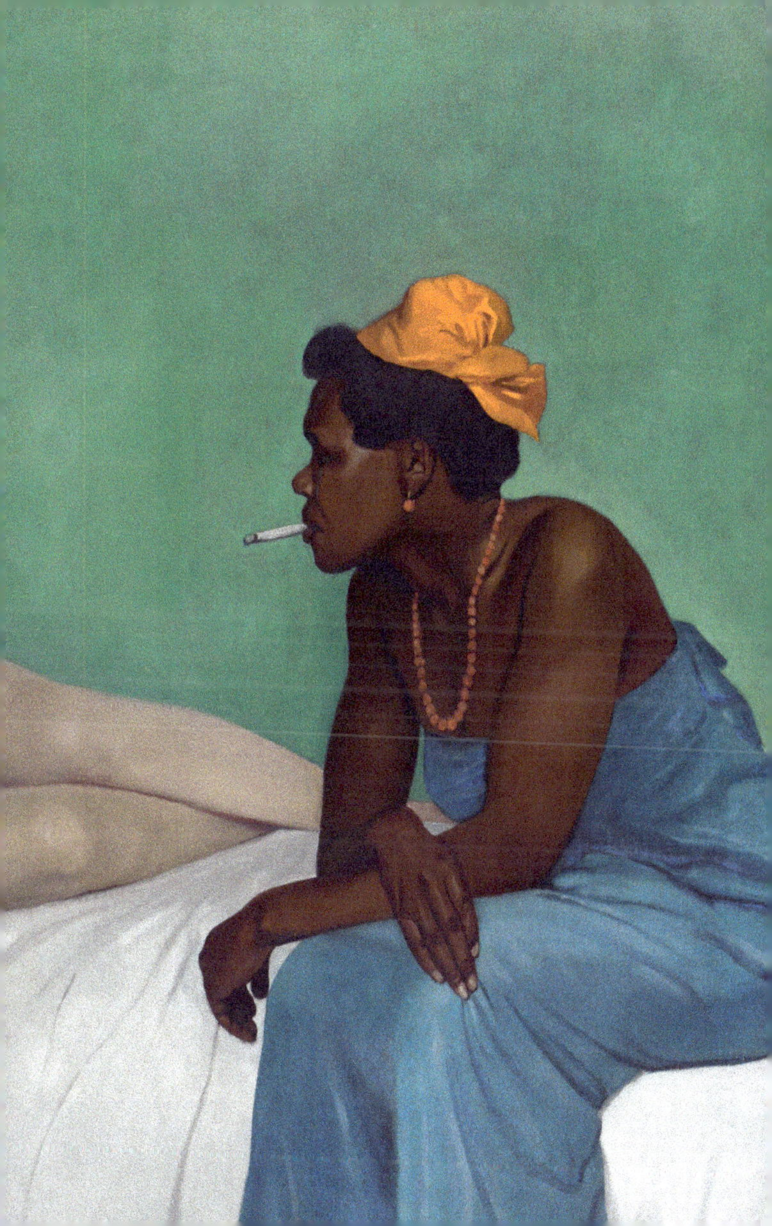

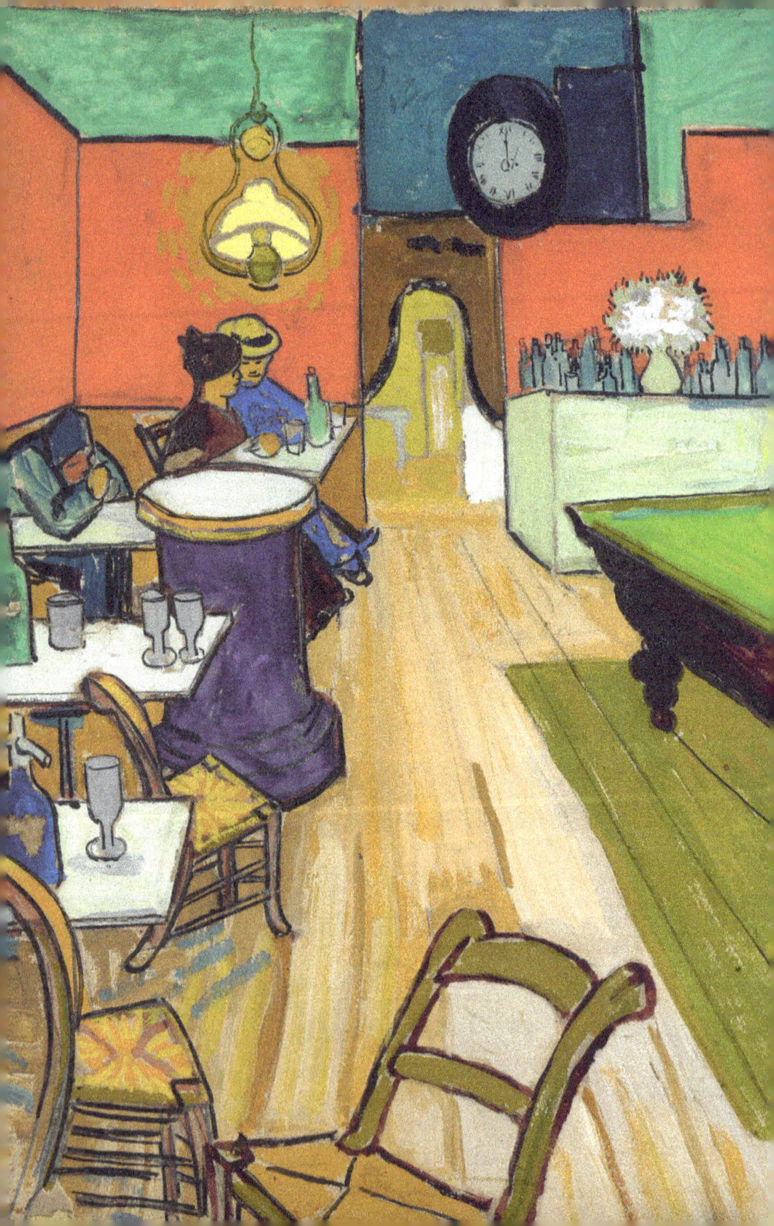

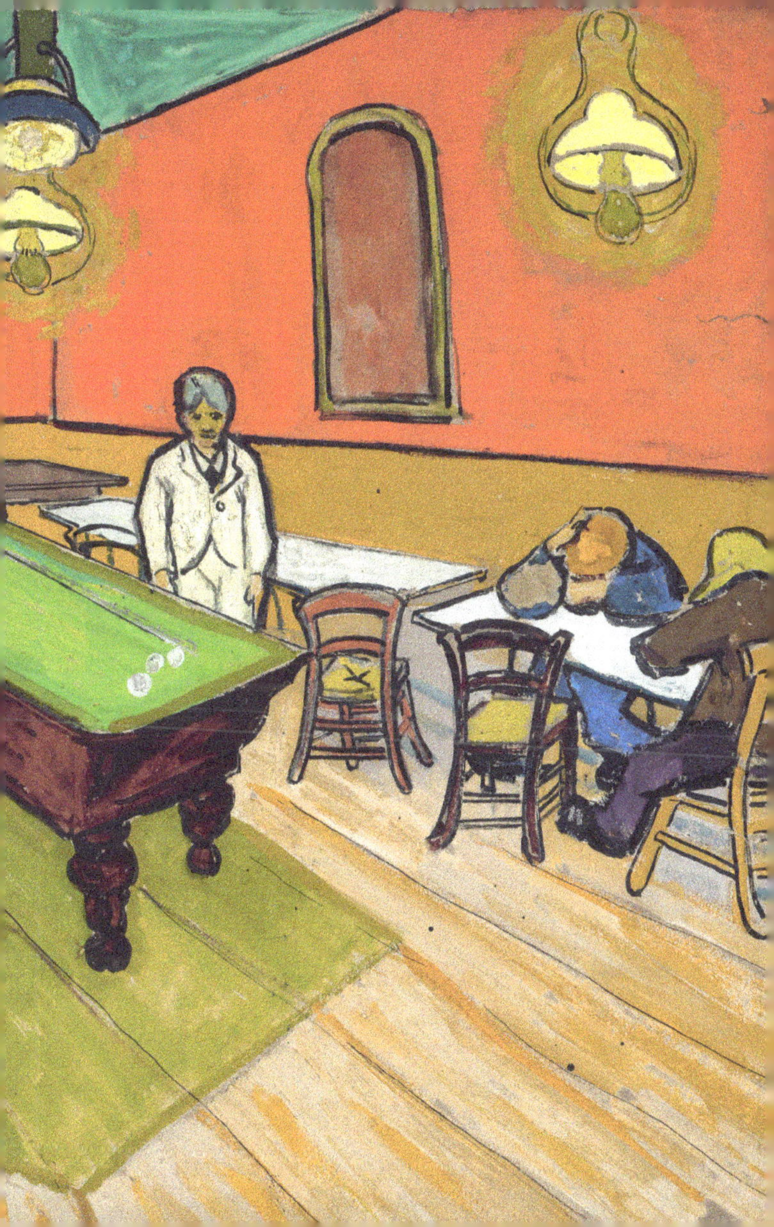

SAMMLUNG OSKAR REINHART "AM RÖMERHOLZ"

— *European classics in a 1920s villa*

In 1924, businessman and patron of the arts Oskar Reinhart did what we'd all like to do: retired early to focus on his large collection of European masters, adding an airy gallery with parquet flooring to his villa for his impressive number of van Goghs, Renoirs, Poussins, Goyas, and friends. Restored to its original design after decades of remodeling, this gallery is also a time capsule of turn-of-the-20th-century private collections, when the affluent bought up moderns to introduce them to an often still-skeptical world. Afterwards, lounge around and enjoy the view of the historic lawns from the terrace of the Café-Bistro "Am Römerholz." Sample traditional Swiss snacks (charcuterie plates) and desserts (fruit tarts) or the lunch special—often meat, greens and carbs with a vegetarian option.

HALDENSTRASSE 95, 8400 WINTERTHUR
ROEMERHOLZ.CH

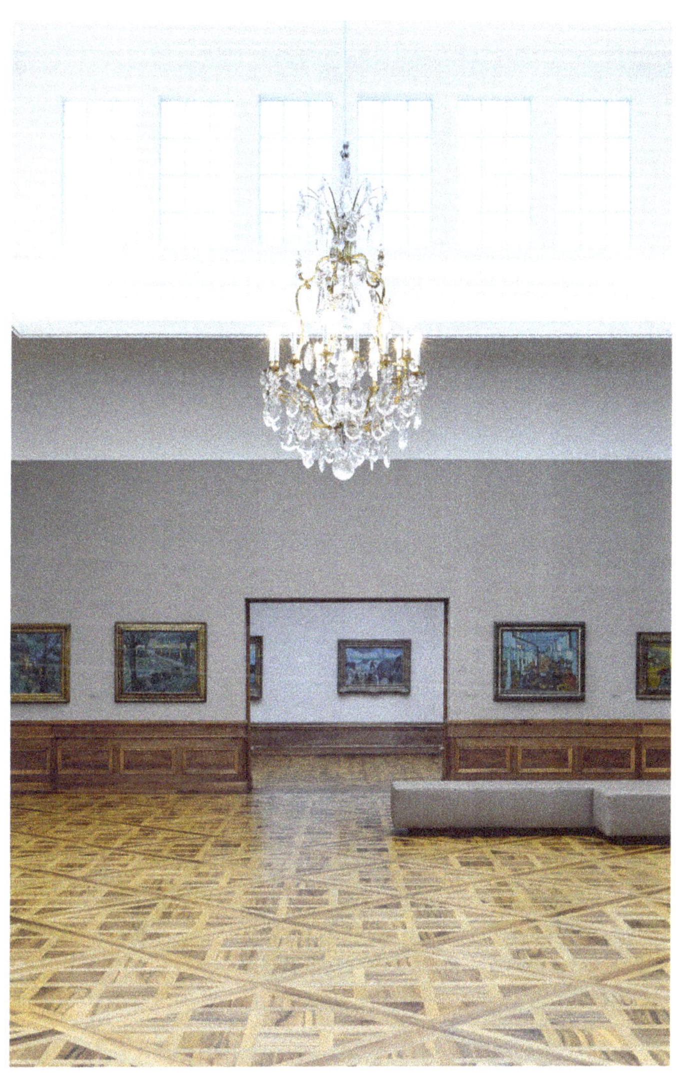

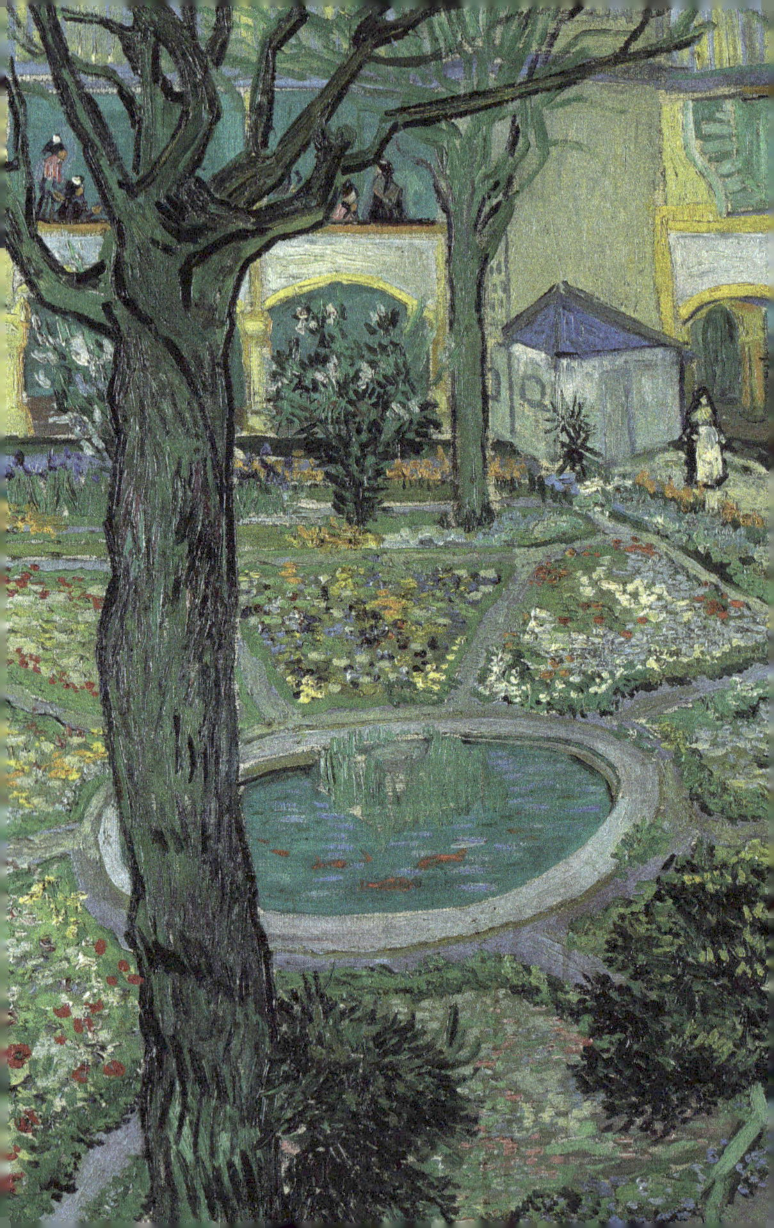

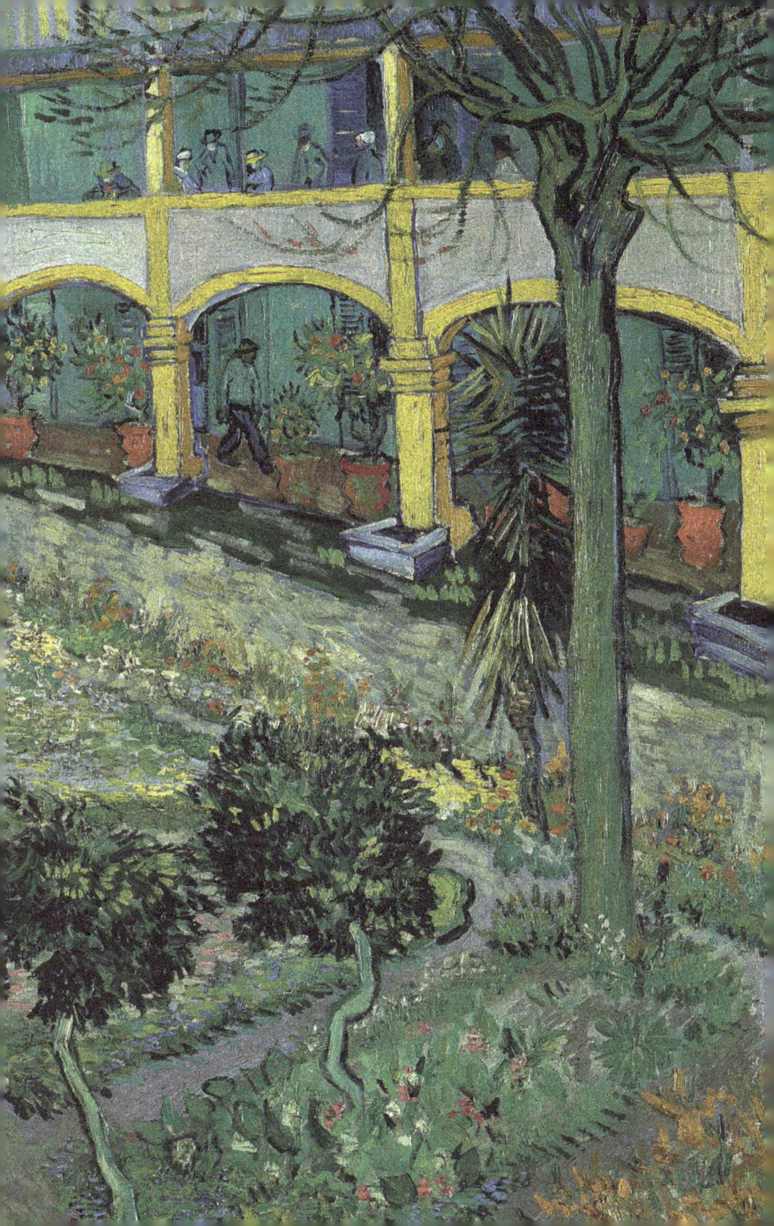

STIFTUNG FÜR KUNST, KULTUR UND GESCHICHTE (SKKG)

— *Making sense of an inheritance*

Imagine inheriting your father's collection of over 100,000 pieces of art—mostly stashed away in dank rooms mere days or weeks after it was purchased, not seeing light for decades. From Giacometti and Hodler paintings to antique shoes and hats; from historic memorabilia—like a toothbrush that reportedly belonged to Napoleon—to World War II weapons like grenades, pistols and a tank. It is dusty, often moldy, sometimes radioactive. Where do you start? Bettina Stefanini has steered her father Bruno's foundation toward a social strategy based on painstaking art restoration, accessibility, provenance research, and a true commitment to the restitution of stolen art. Although the SKKG does not plan to open a physical museum, it does lend pieces to others. A future project foresees the collection going online and an exhibition space is being built for selected pieces—see website for details.

SKKG.CH

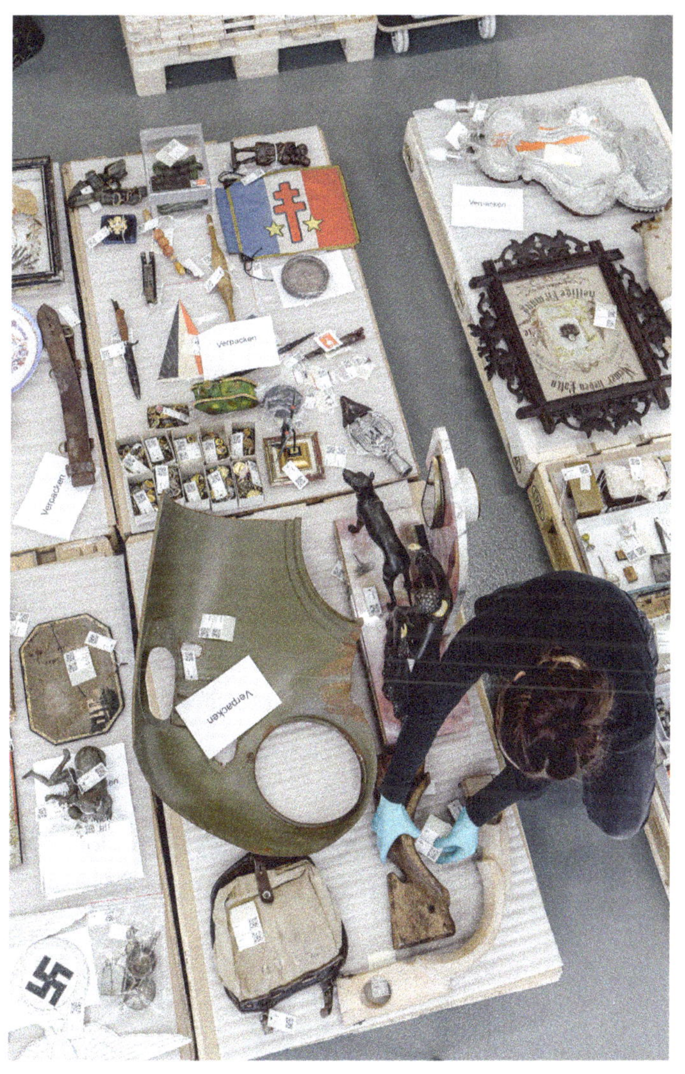
Verpacken
Verpacken
Verpacken
Verpacken

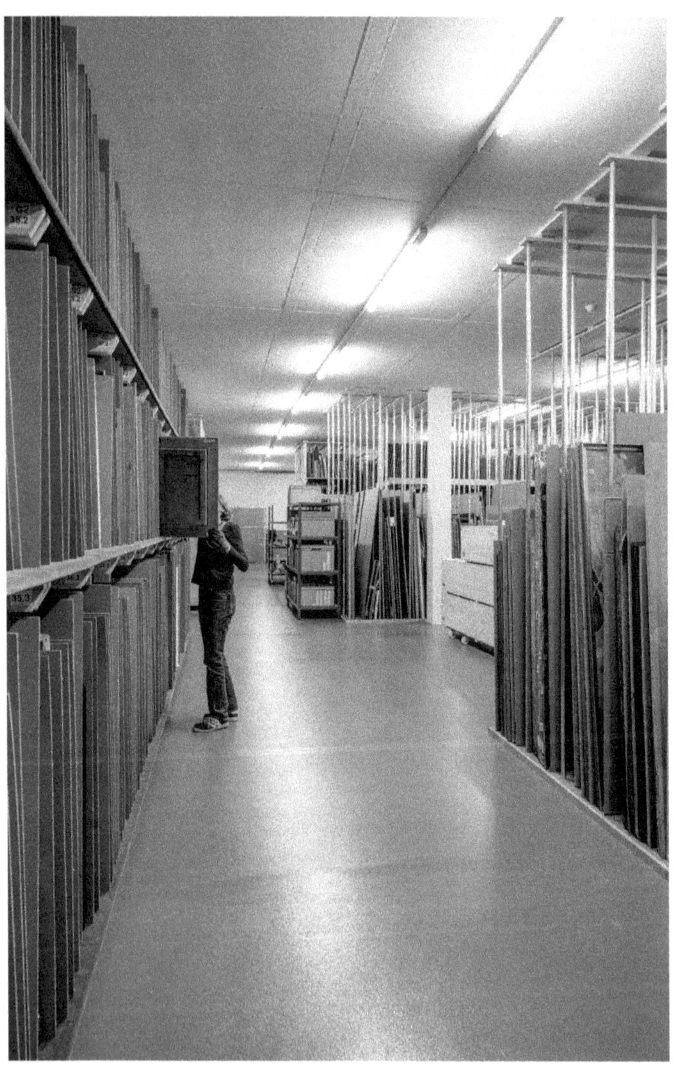

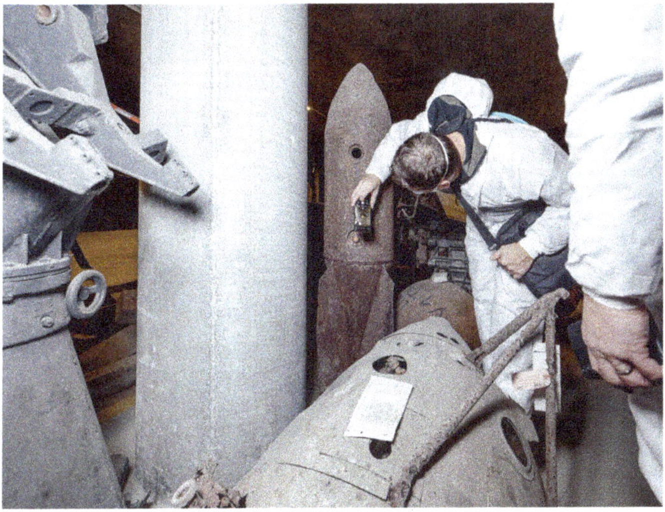

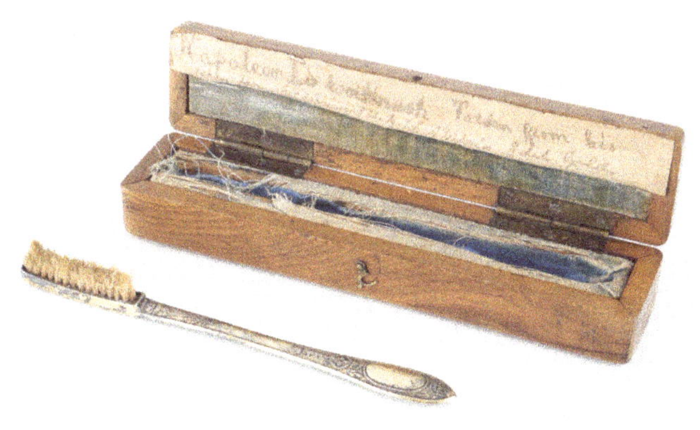

LÖWENBRÄUKUNST -AREAL

— *Zurich's hub for 20th- and 21st-century art*

Over the past 30 years, the former Löwenbräu brewery has transformed into a collection of museums and private galleries. Haus Konstruktiv focuses on constructivist-concrete and conceptual art. Its highlight is Fritz Glarner's "Rockefeller Dining Room," which he designed for the home of the American businessman Nelson Rockefeller in 1963/64. The innovative Kunsthalle Zürich, which experiments with installations by international artists like Maggie Lee, Ana Jotta and Pippa Garner, is one of the few art museums in Switzerland that gives equal weight to exhibitions by all genders. The Migros Museum für Gegenwartskunst (contemporary art; free admission) was founded by the Swiss retailer and is financed by its program which donates a percentage of its revenue to cultural and social initiatives. It commissioned the phenomenal, internationally acclaimed installation and video art piece "The Visitors" by Ragnar Kjartansson.

LIMMATSTRASSE 268–270, 8005 ZURICH
HAUSKONSTRUKTIV.CH
KUNSTHALLEZURICH.CH
MIGROSMUSEUM.CH

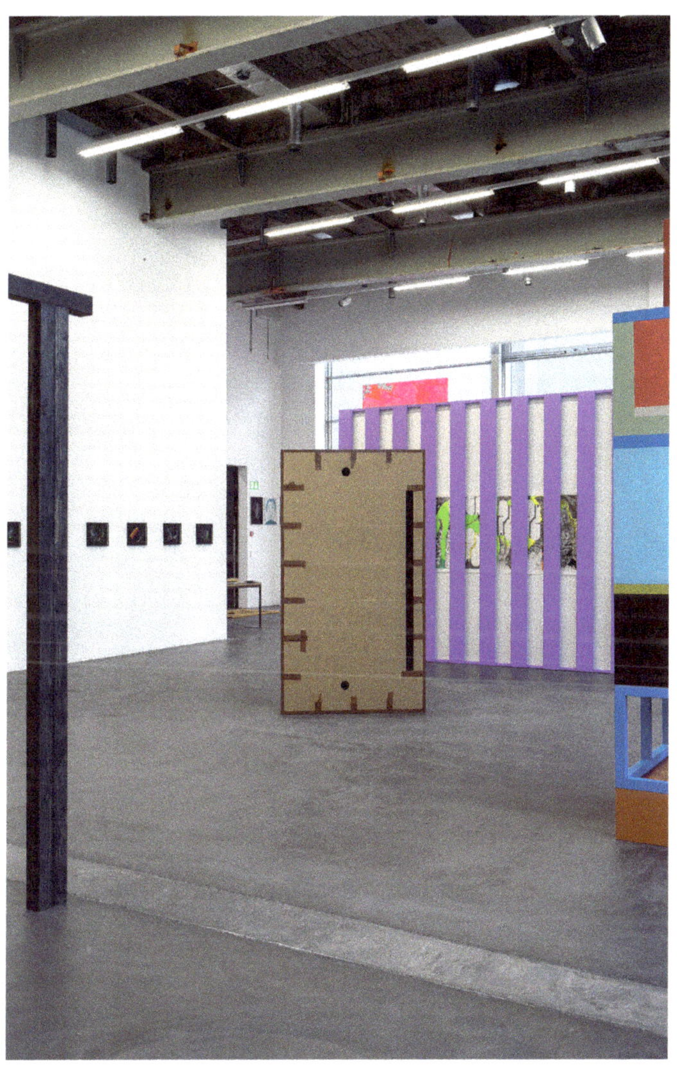

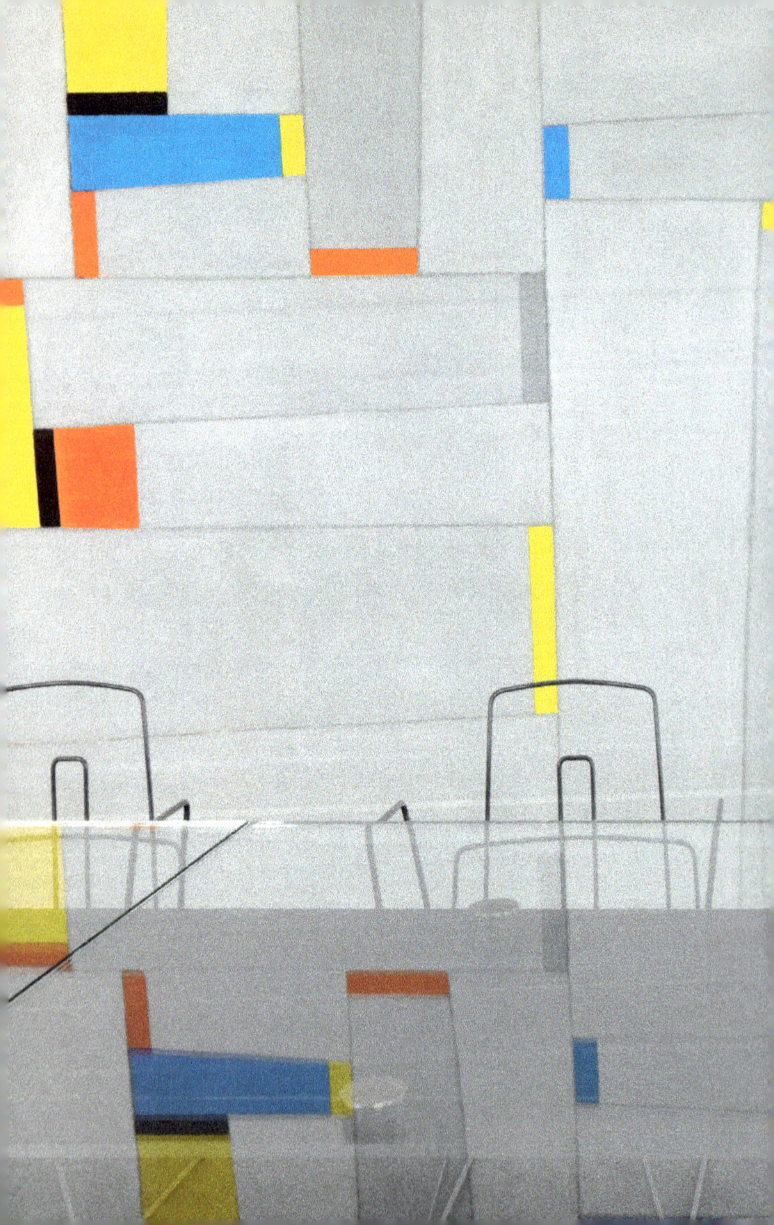

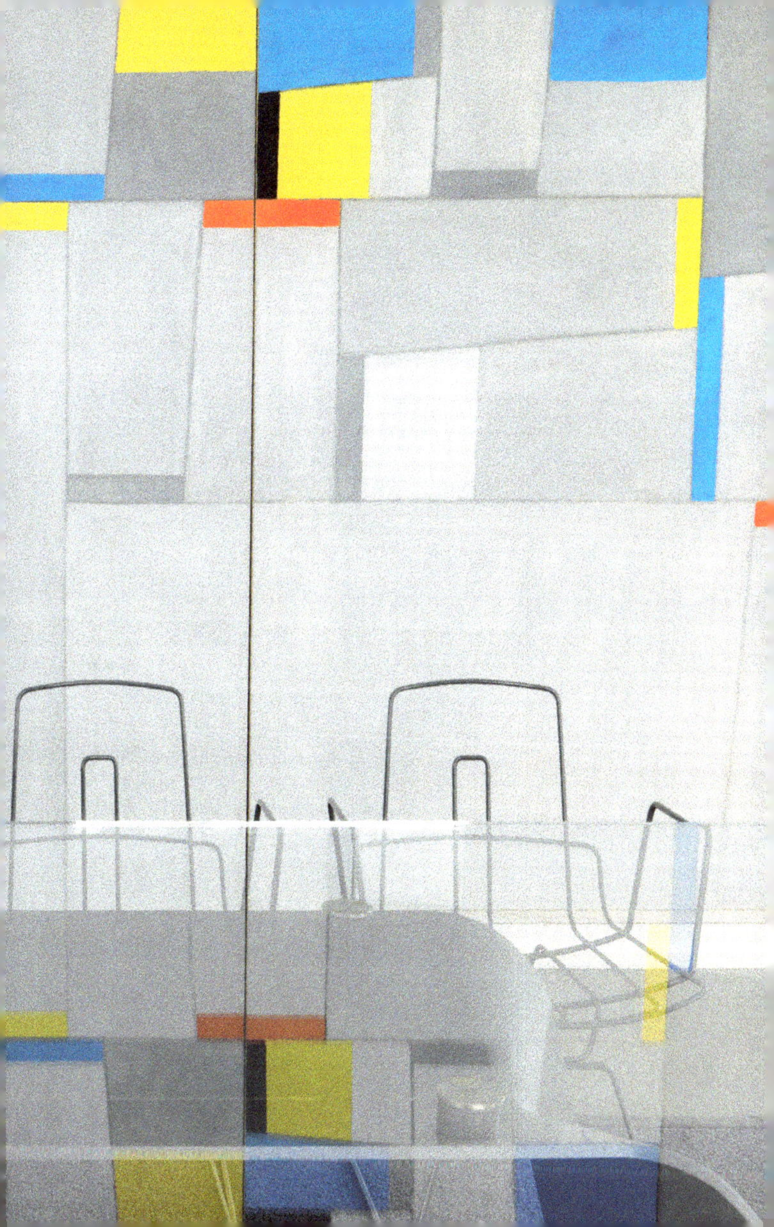

KUNSTHAUS ZÜRICH

— *The classic*

The Kunsthaus is a Zurich institution founded and still run by an association that anyone can join. Doubled in size thanks to the 2020 Chipperfield addition across Heimplatz, with an underground passage linking the two, it's generally packed on cold or rainy Sundays. This is a one-stop European art extravaganza with works from the Middle Ages through to the present day. Get up to speed on Swiss artists (Füssli, Hodler, Giacometti, Rist, Fischli/Weiss, Taeuber-Arp), discover oh-that's-where-the-original-is (post)impressionists (Monet, Manet, van Gogh), and browse through the contemporaries (Sherman, Polke, Attia, Bernstein). The kiddies can be stashed in a hands-on creative workshop while you saunter past masterpieces on your way to the Kunsthausbar, where refined plating flourishes are as important as local, seasonal lentils and co.

HEIMPLATZ 1/5, 8001 ZURICH
KUNSTHAUS.CH

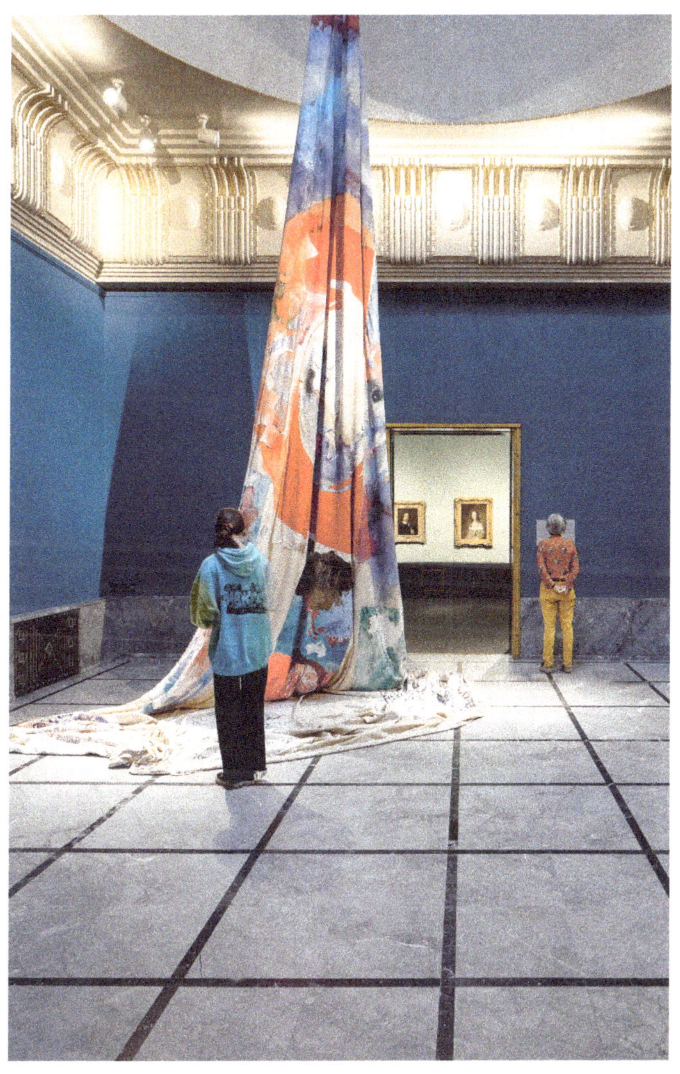

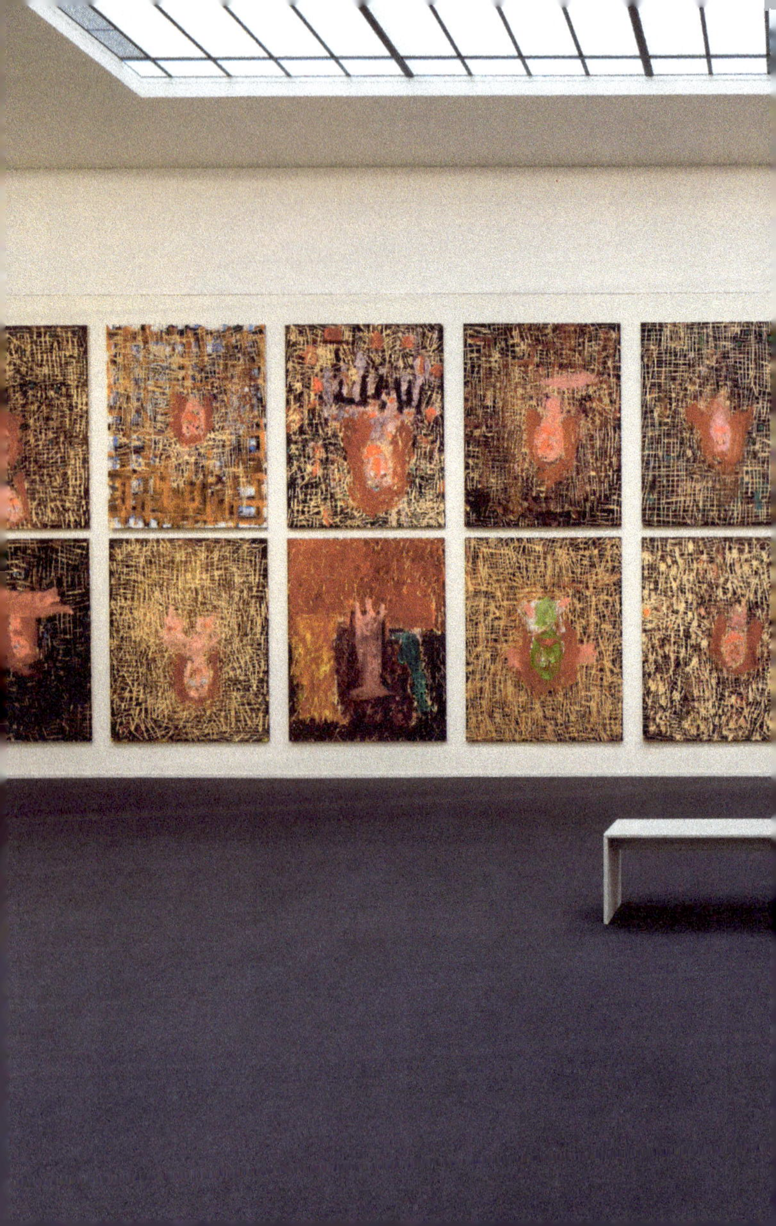

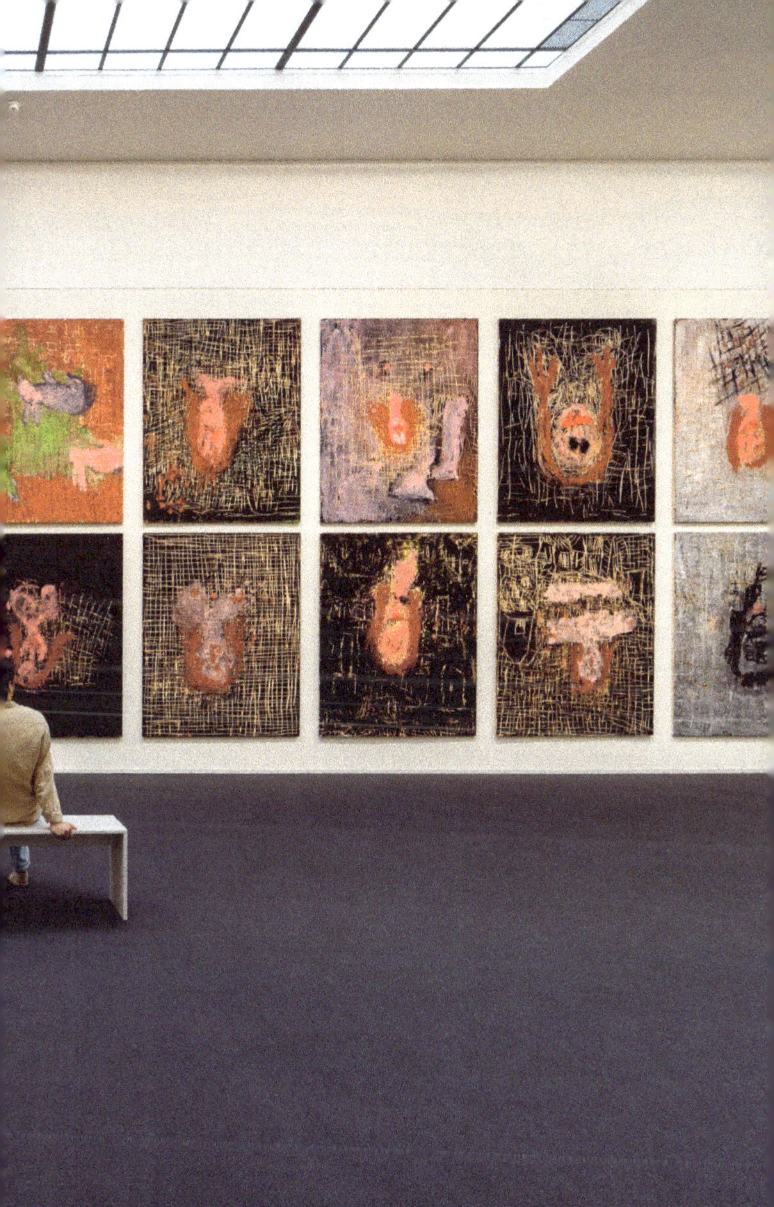

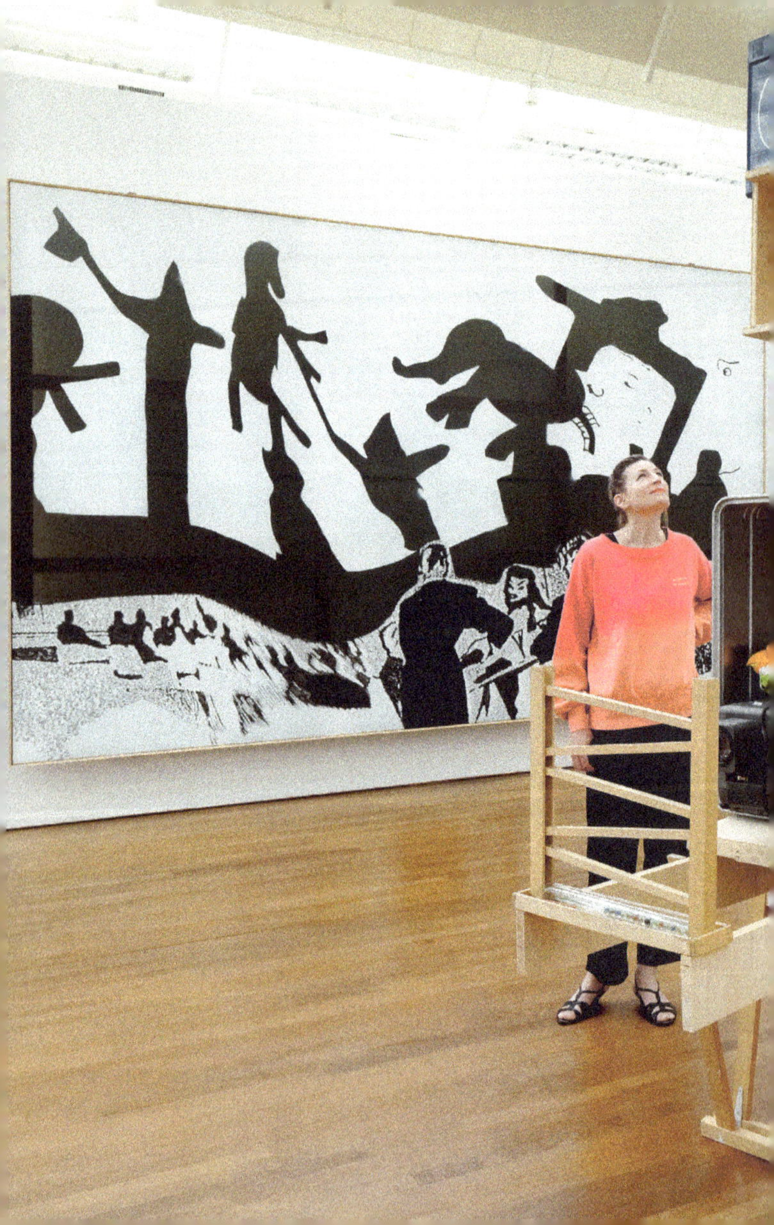

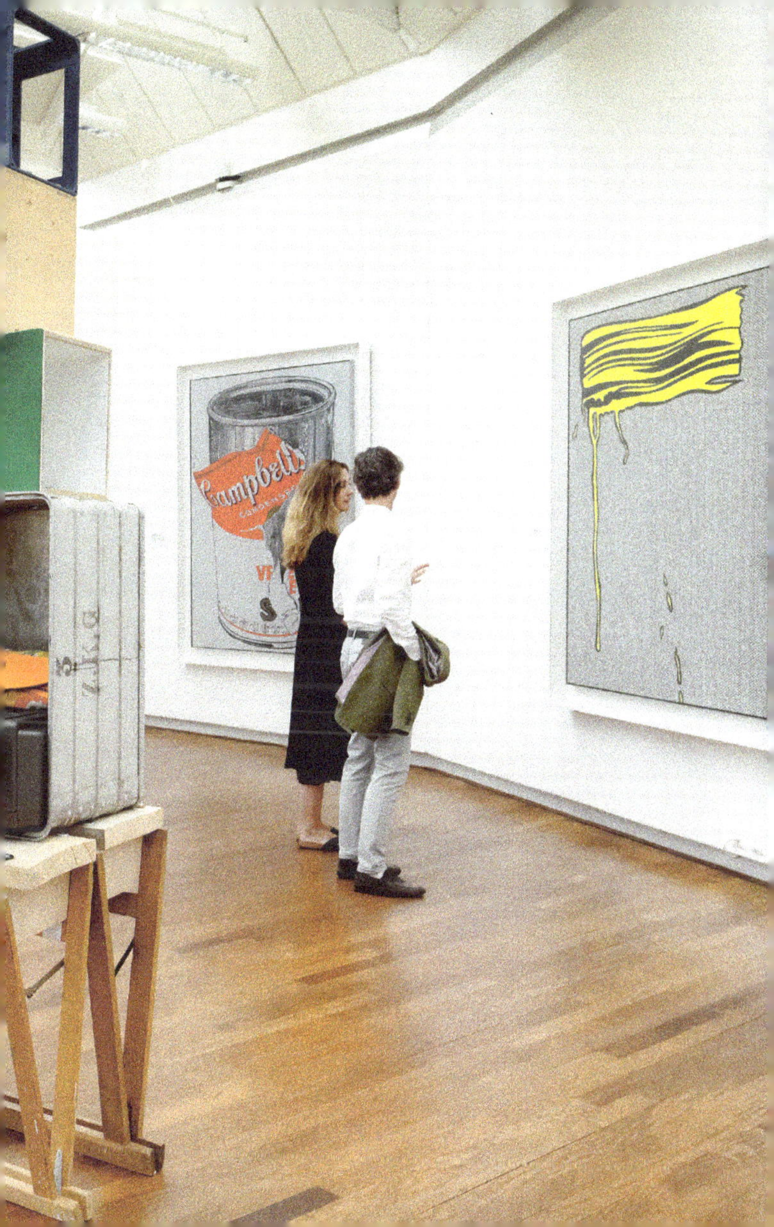
Campbell's

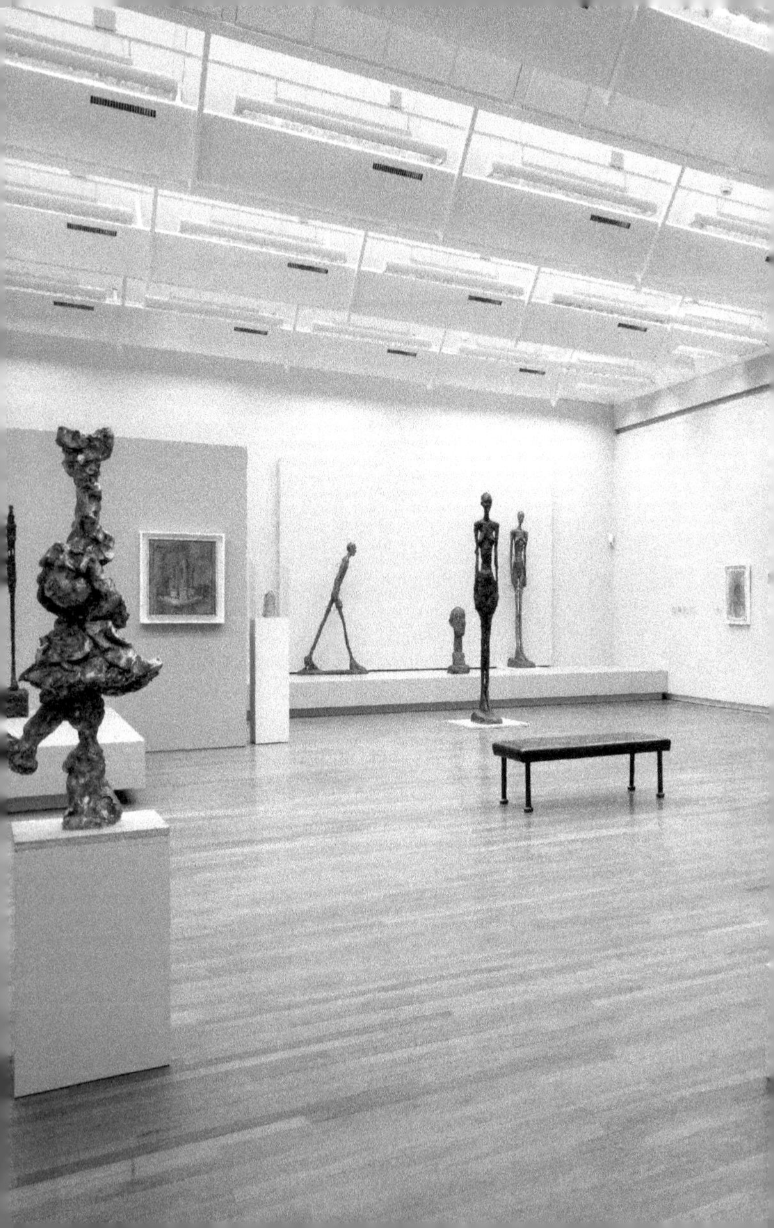

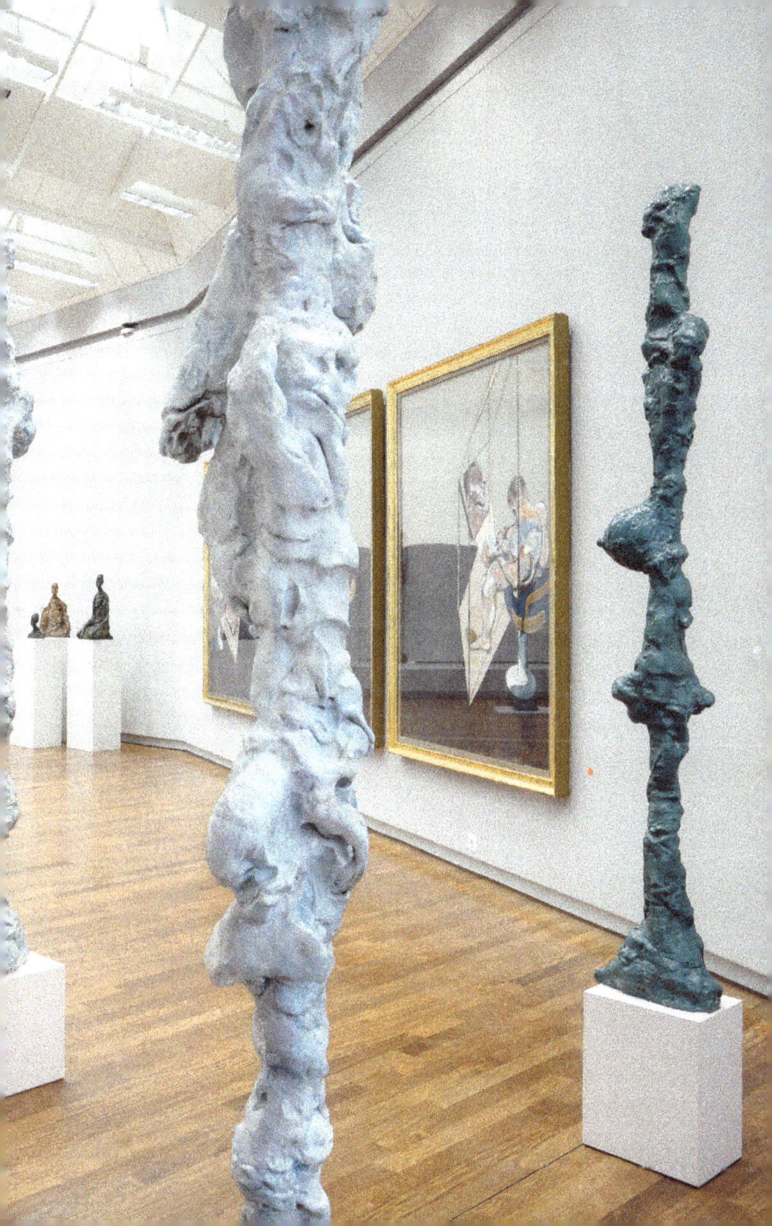

MUSEUM RIETBERG

— *Switzerland's largest museum of non-European art*

The tranquil public Rieterpark on the edge of Zurich contains the Villas Schönberg, Rieter and Wesendonck. The latter, where guest Richard Wagner dallied with his host's wife as he wrote some of his famous works, was the museum's original location until 2007. Today, the main entrance—called the *Smaragd*, or emerald, thanks to its striking green facade—leads to a modern underground addition that's home to most of the museum's temporary and permanent installations. A highlight of the Rietberg's Asian, African, American, and Oceanian art is the Meiyintang Collection of 600 Chinese ceramics, bronzes and porcelain—considered one of the finest on display in the Western world. The gift shop is stuffed with books if you have more questions. The self-serve café makes good, light meals and snacks in what used to be the Villa Wesendonck's conservatory. There is no public parking and rare availability on the surrounding streets.

GABLERSTRASSE 15, 8002 ZURICH
RIETBERG.CH

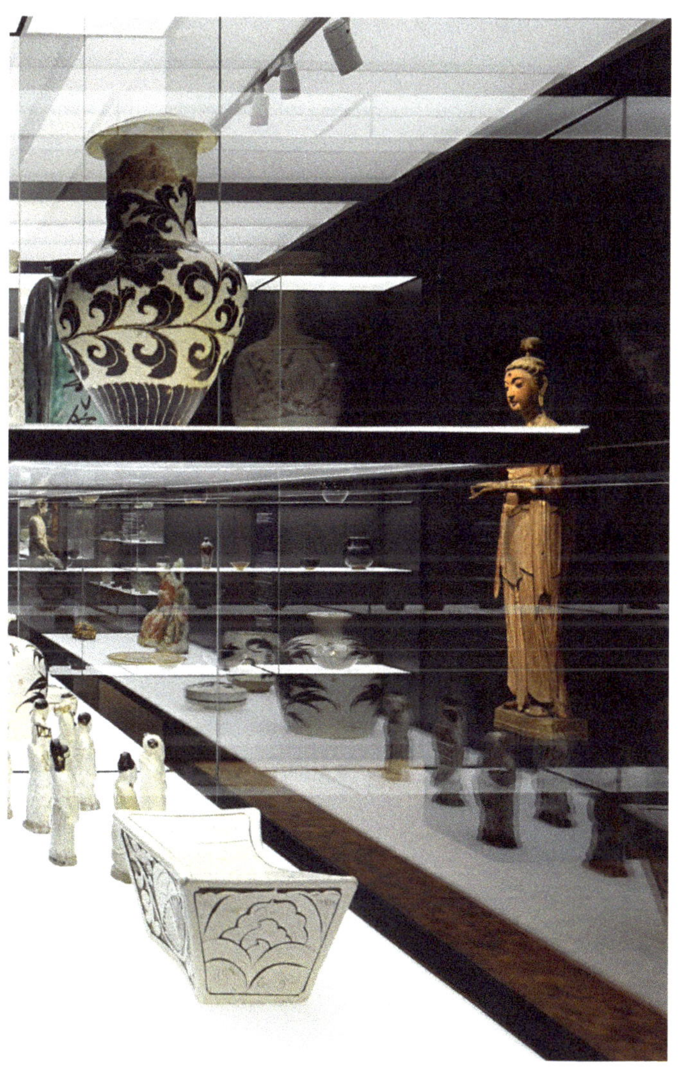

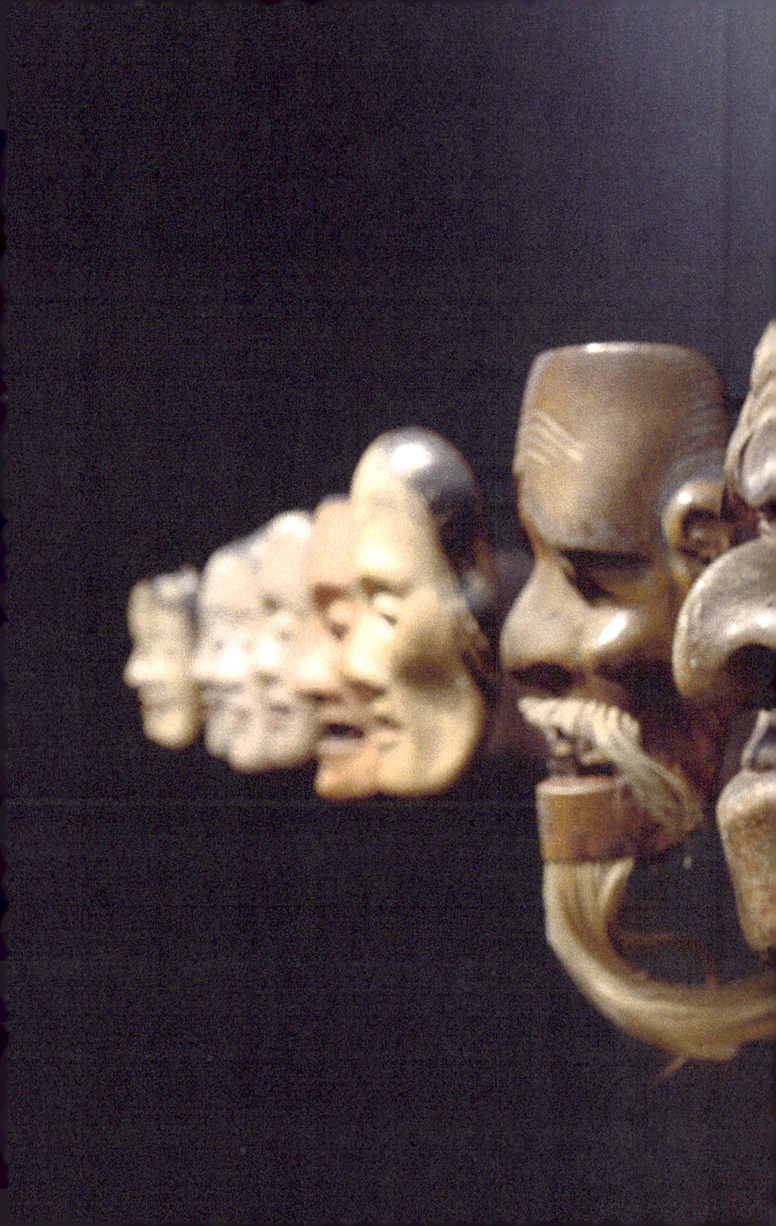

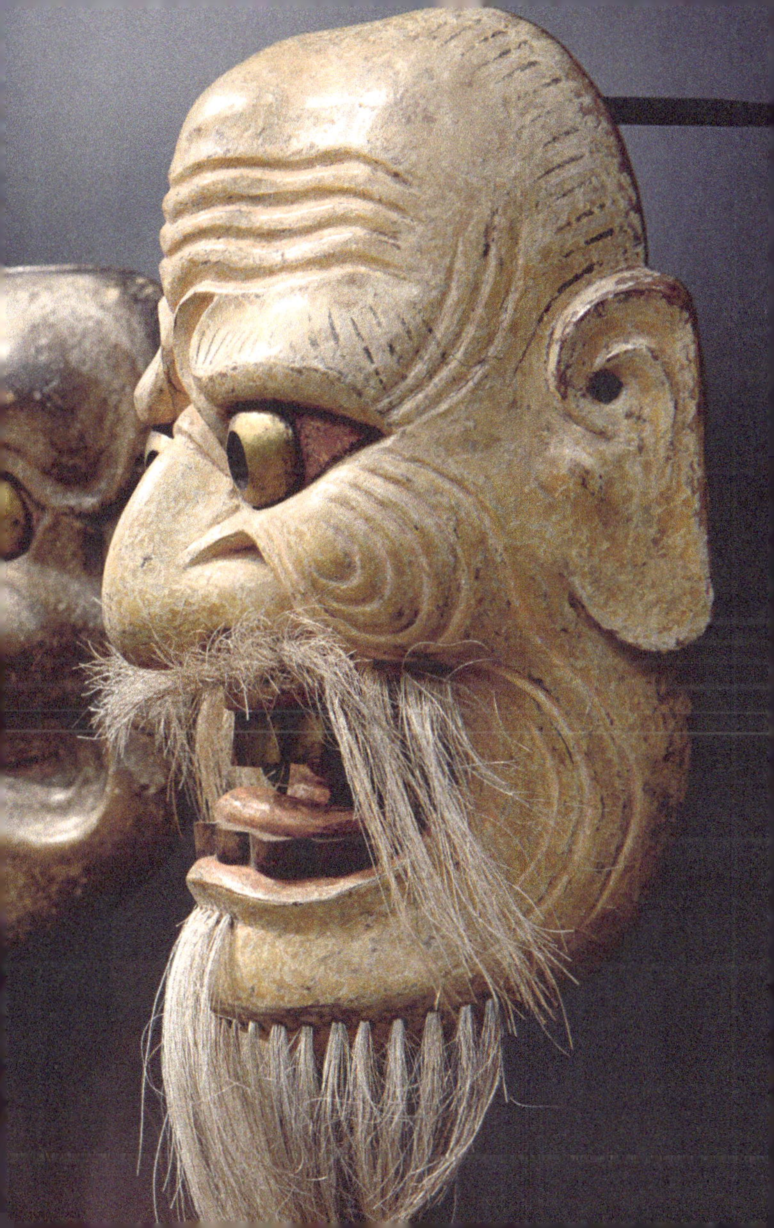

MUSEUM FÜR GESTALTUNG ZÜRICH

— *Switzerland's leading design museum*

A magnet for design lovers, the museum of Zurich University of the Arts is split into two locations. The original site at Ausstellungsstrasse is a listed building: a superb example of modern Swiss architecture featuring special exhibitions and the Swiss Design Lounge where, as the name suggests, lounging is encouraged. The Toni-Areal location is home to the museum's four collections—design, graphics, decorative arts, and posters—boasting over 500,000 objects that include works by Alice Bailly, Magdalena Abakanowicz and Cristóbal Balenciaga. The pieces were, and still are, collected by the university for teaching purposes. The gift shops at both sites are fabulous for unique design finds and limited editions. Take a piece of lemon loaf from the Ausstellungsstrasse café out to the adjacent park or warm up with a homemade hot soup-and-sandwich combo at a sleek indoor table.

AUSSTELLUNGSSTRASSE 60, 8005 ZURICH
TONI-AREAL: PFINGSTWEIDSTRASSE 96, 8005 ZURICH
MUSEUM-GESTALTUNG.CH

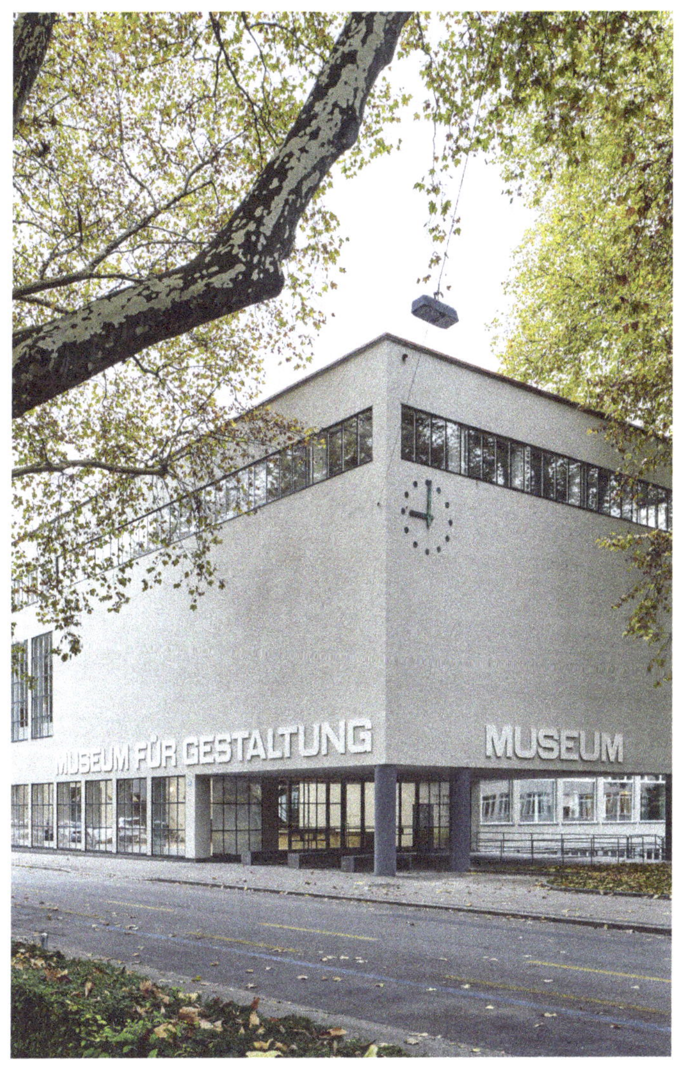
MUSEUM FÜR GESTALTUNG
MUSEUM

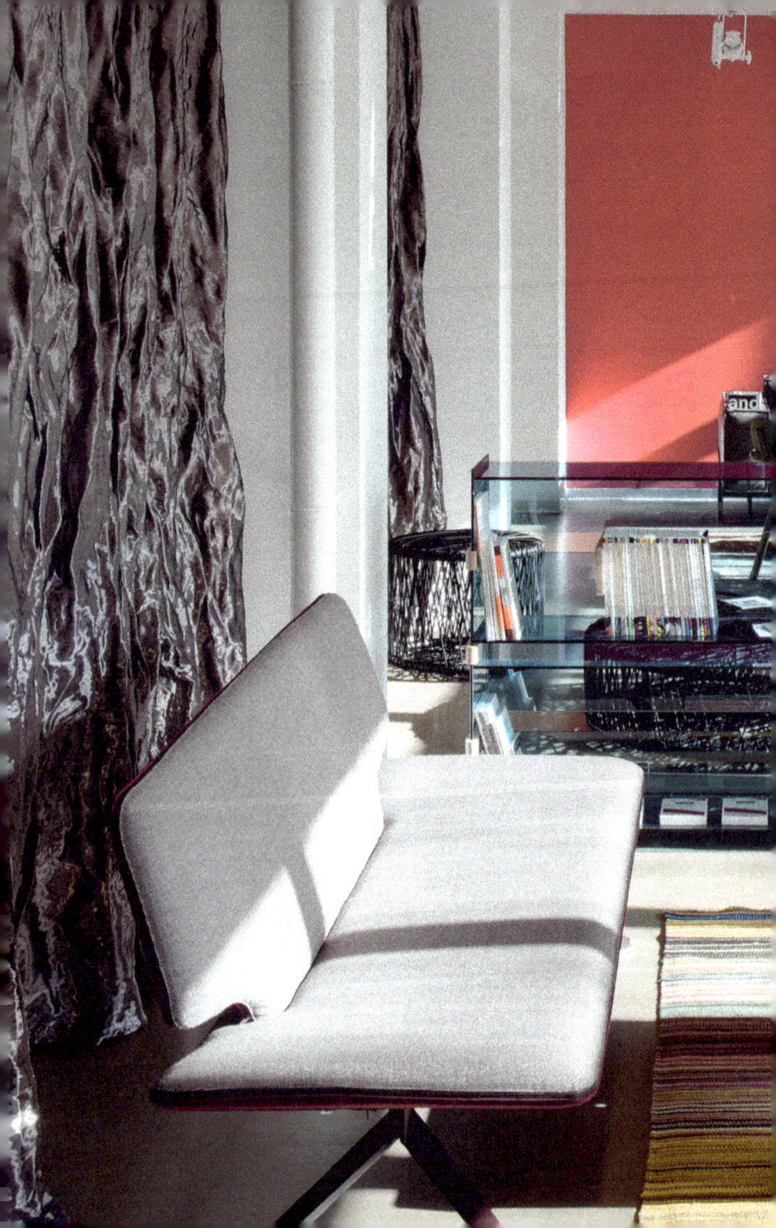
and

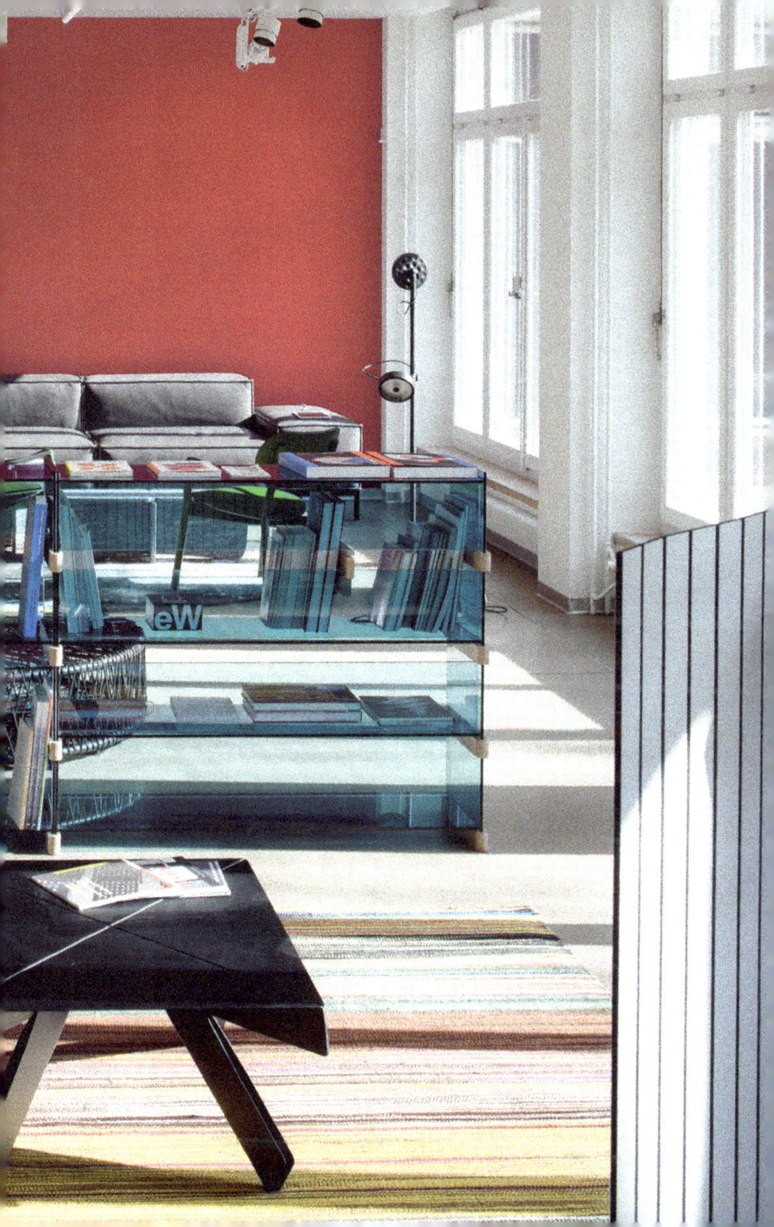

IMAGE

p.7: Sarah Brahim, Untitled, inkjet print, 2023. Photo: Andrea Rossetti for Bally Foundation Villa Heleneum; p.9: © René Rötheli, Baden; p.11: Pierre-Auguste Renoir, Der Zopf, Um 1886/87, Oil on canvas, 57 x 47 cm. © Museum Langmatt, Baden; pp.12–13: Pierre-Auguste Renoir, The Boat, 1878, Oil on canvas, 54.5 x 65.5 cm. © Museum Langmatt, Baden; p.15: Fake_Yellow Corridor: The Office for the Whole Truth, from the FAKE exhibition. © Stapferhaus/Thijs Wolzak; pp.16–17: Geschlecht_982: Geschlechtsorgane: Ein Varieté zu Faszination und Scham. © Stapferhaus/Anita Affentranger; p.19: Francisco Sierra, Kunsthalle-Appenzell. Photo: Sebastien Verdon. © Heinrich Gebert Kulturstiftung Appenzell; pp.20–21: Exhibition view, Alice Channer, Kunsthaus-Appenzell. Photo: Roman März. © Heinrich Gebert Kulturstiftung Appenzell; p.23: Lucas Cranach d. Ä. The Judgement of Paris. Image in the public domain—Kunstmuseum Basel; pp.24–25: Ernst Ludwig Kirchner. Stafelalp, Return of the Animals. Image in the public domain—Kunstmuseum Basel; p.27: Both photos © Katrin Gygax; p.29: Museum Tinguely (view from the south) © 2023 Museum Tinguely Basel. Photo: Daniel Spehr; pp.30–31: Interior view of the "barca" with a view of the Rhine and the city © 2023 Museum Tinguely Basel. Photo: Pino Musi; p.33: © Katrin Gygax; pp.35–37: Photos: Andreas Zimmermann/von Bartha; p:39: Paul Klee. Zeichen in Gelb, 1937. Pastel on cotton. 83.5 x 50.3 cm. Fondation Beyeler, Riehen/Basel, Sammlung Beyeler. Photo: Robert Bayer; p.40: Kasimir Malewitsch. Suprematistische Komposition, 1915. Öl auf Leinwand, 80.4 x 80.6 cm. Fondation Beyeler, Riehen/Basel, Sammlung Beyeler. Photo: Robert Bayer; p.41: Wassily Kandinsky. Fuga, 1914. Öl auf Leinwand, 129.5 x 129.5 cm. Fondation Beyeler, Riehen/Basel, Sammlung Beyeler. Photo: Robert Bayer; p.43: WikiMedia: https://commons.wikimedia.org/wiki/File:Zentrum_Paul_Klee_(622816449).jpg; p.45: © Katrin Gygax; p.49: © Katrin Gygax; p.51: Helene Pflugshaupt, Zwischen Hell und Dunkel, 1957. Oil on canvas, 77.7 x 52.8 cm. Photo by Christian Helmle. © Kunstmuseum Thun; pp.52–53: Chantal Michel, Die Kunst wird von der Politik getragen, 2004. Lambda print on Alucobond. 80 x 120 cm. Photo by Christian Helmle. © Kunstmuseum Thun; Christian Helmle, Lichtmensch, 1983/1984. Photography. 40 x 50 cm. Photo by Christian Helmle. © Kunstmuseum Thun; p.55: Interior, staircase. Photo: Flora Bevilacqua. © MAH Genève; pp.56–57: Interior, Italian Baroque. Photo: Flora Bevilacqua. © MAH Genève; pp.59–61: © Katrin Gygax; p.63: Angelika Kauffmann (1741–1807). Cleone trauert um ihren Sohn, 1781. Oil on copper. 31 x 26 cm. Bündner Kunstmuseum Chur, Gift of Dr. Johannes Fulda, Maienfeld/Kilchberg, 2021; pp.64–65: Angelika Kauffmann (1741–1807). Die Bacchantinnen, from 1786. Oil on copper. 22 x 27.5 cm.

Bündner Kunstmuseum Chur, Gift of Dr. Johannes Fulda, Maienfeld/Kilchberg, 2021; p.67: Magdalena Abakanowicz. Flock I (1990). © Studio Stefano Graziani for Muzeum Susch/ Art Stations Foundation CH. Courtesy of The Marta Magdalena Abakanowicz-Kosmowska and Jan Kosmowski Foundation; pp.68–69: Mirosław Bałka. NARCISSUSSUSCH (2018). © Studio Stefano Graziani for Muzeum Susch/Art Stations Foundation CH; p.71: Auguste Renoir. L'Italienne au Tambourin 1881. © Museum Sammlung Rosengart, Lucerne; pp.72–73: Paul Klee. Kristallinische Landschaft, 1929. © Museum Sammlung Rosengart, Lucerne; p.75: Hans Holbein (the Younger). Solothurner Madonna, 1522. Oil on lime wood. 143.5 x 102 x 3.7 cm. Übernommen vom Kunstverein Solothurn, 1879. Photo: David Aebi; p.76: Eva Aeppli. Honoré, 1974. Stoffplastik, Stuhl. 130 x 85 x 95 cm. Gift of Meret Oppenheim, 1974. © Susanne Gyger, Lucerne. Photo: SIK-ISEA, Zurich; p.77: Cuno Amiet. The yellow hill, 1903. Tempera on fabric. 98 x 72 cm. Dübi-Müller-Stiftung. © D. Thalmann, Aarau, Switzerland. Photo: SIK-ISEA, Zurich; p.81: © Katrin Gygax; p.83: Sarah Brahim. The second sound of an echo, 2 channels video, 2023. Photo: Andrea Rossetti; pp.84–85: Sarah Brahim. Sometimes we are all eternal, 2023. Photo: Andrea Rossetti; p.87: MASI Lugano, Bianco o nero. Photo: Alfio Tommasini. © MASI Lugano; pp.88–89: MASI Lugano. Photo: Luca Meneghel. © MASI Lugano; p.91: Henry Moore. Large Reclining Figure, 1982. © Michel Darbellay, Fondation Pierre Gianadda; pp.93–95: Museum HR Giger. Photos: Matthias Belz. © HR Giger Museum; pp.96–97: Museum HR Giger, Giger-Bar. Photo: Andy Davies. © HR Giger Museum; p.99: Vue intérieure de la Collection de l'Art Brut, Lausanne. Photo: Delphine Burtin. Archives de la Collection de l'Art Brut, Lausanne; Vue intérieure de la Collection de l'Art Brut, Lausanne. Photo: Caroline Smyrliadis. Archives de la Collection de l'Art Brut, Lausanne; p.101: mudac: A Chair and You. © Lucy Jansch; p.102: mudac and Photo Elysée buildings, Plateforme 10. © Matthieu Gafsou; p.103: mudac: Dialogue between an octopus and a citrus press, 2023. © Etienne Malapert; p.105: © Photo Fondation de l'Hermitage; pp.107–109: © Musée national suisse; p.113: © Katrin Gygax; p.115: Vinci. Photo: Maria Anna Weber; p.117: © Galerie Bruno Bischofberger; pp.119–121: Visualisation of the new Fotomuseum Winterthur © Nightnurse Images/RWPA; p.123: Giovanni Giacometti. Bildnis Ottilia Giacometti, 1912. Oil on canvas, 61 x 50 cm. Rahmenmass: 77 x 65.5 x 6.5 cm. © Kunst Museum Winterthur, Stiftung Oskar Reinhart; pp.124–125: Félix Vallotton. La blanche et la noire, 1913. Oil on canvas, 114 x 147 cm Rahmenmass: 138 x 169.5 x 8 cm. © Kunst Museum Winterthur, Hahnloser/Jaeggli Stiftung; pp.126–127: Vincent van Gogh.

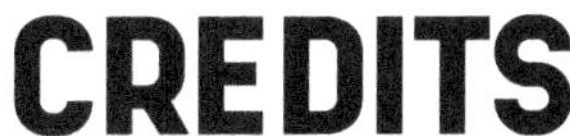

Le café de nuit à Arles, 1888. Bleistift, Wasserfarben und Deckfarben auf Papier auf Karton, 44.4 x 63.2 cm Rahmenmass: 70.5 x 87.6 x 8.3 cm. © Kunst Museum Winterthur, Hahnloser/Jaeggli Stiftung; p.129: The Grand Gallery Interior. © Sammlung Oskar Reinhart «Am Römerholz», Winterthur; pp.130–131: Vincent van Gogh. The Courtyard of the Hospital at Arles, 1889. Oil on canvas. © Sammlung Oskar Reinhart «Am Römerholz», Winterthur; pp.133–134: Photos Bruno Augsburger. © SKKG 2021; p.135: Photo: Bruno Augsburger. © SKKG 2021; Photo: ©SKKG 2021; p.137: Exhibition view, Zurich Biennale 2023. Photo: Cedric Mussano. © Kunsthalle Zürich; pp.138–139: Fritz Glarner, The Rockefeller Dining Room, 1963/1964. Oil on canvas. Sammlung Museum Haus Konstruktiv, gift of Paul Büchi Stiftung. Photo: Stefan Altenburger. © Haus Konstruktiv; p.141: Kunsthaus Zürich, Interventionsraum: Anna Boghiguian, Untitled, 2018; Kader Attia, Culture, Another Nature Repaired, 2018. © Anna Boghiguian; © 2021, ProLitteris, Zurich. Photo: Franca Candrian, Kunsthaus Zürich; pp.142–143: Kunsthaus Zürich, Georg Baselitz. Photo © Franca Candrian, Kunsthaus Zürich. Artwork © Georg Baselitz; Kunsthaus Zürich, Sammlung Knecht. Photo: Franca Candrian, Kunsthaus Zürich; pp.144–145: Kunsthaus Zürich, Pop Art und zeitgenössische Kunst. Photo: © Franca Candrian, Kunsthaus Zürich; Works: © Abraham Cruzvillegas; © The Andy Warhol Foundation for the Visual Arts, Inc./2023, ProLitteris, Zurich; © Estate of Roy Lichtenstein/2023, ProLitteris, Zurich; © The Estate of Sigmar Polke, Cologne/2023, ProLitteris, Zurich; pp.146–147: Kunsthaus Zürich, Alberto Giacometti and Rebecca Warren. © Succession, Alberto Giacometti/2021 ProLitteris, Zurich; © Rebecca Warren, Photo: Franca Candrian, Kunsthaus Zürich; p.149: Meiyintang Collection. Photo: © Museum Rietberg; pp.150–151: Masks, Japan. Photo: © Museum Rietberg; p.153: Museum für Gestaltung Zürich, Ausstellungsstrasse building, 2017. © Photo: Georg Aerni; pp.154–155: Museum für Gestaltung Zürich, exhibition Swiss Design Lounge, 2018, © ZHdK; p.159: Pierre-Auguste Renoir. Sleeping Girl. Oil on canvas. © Sammlung Oskar Reinhart «Am Römerholz», Winterthur.

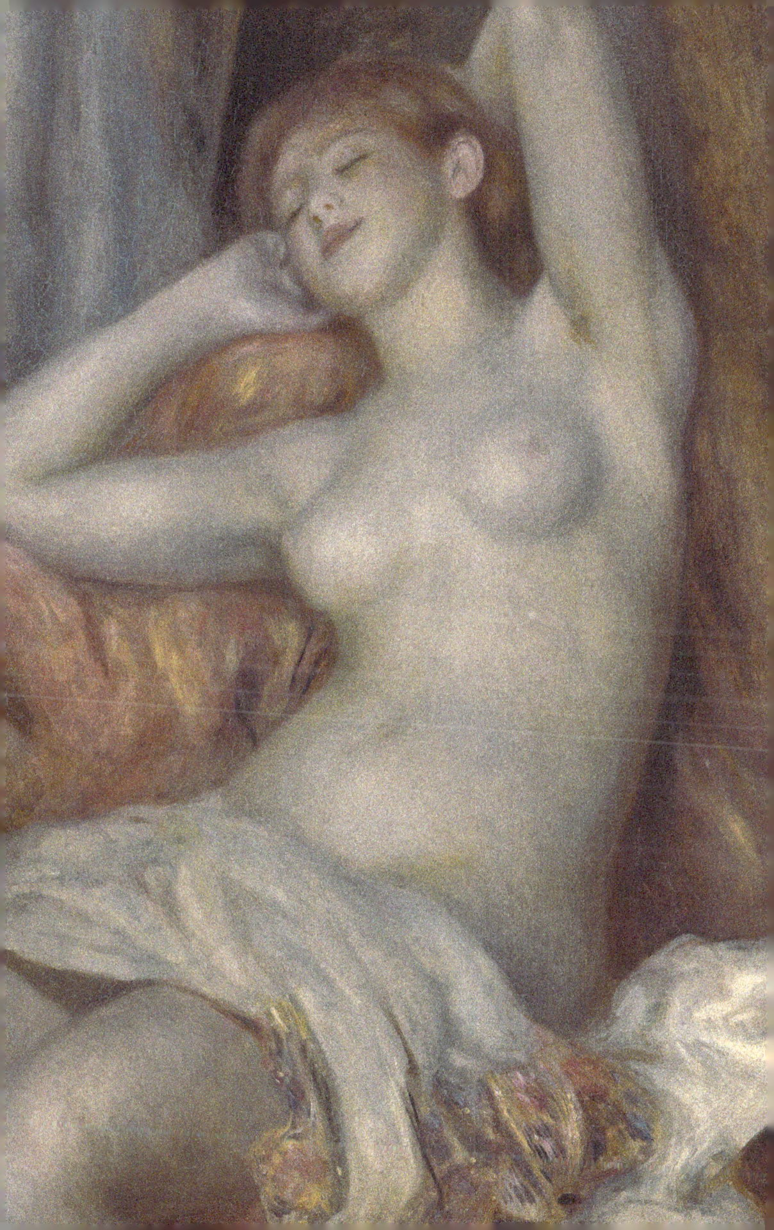

ABOUT THE

Katrin Gygax works in Zurich as a travel writer, editor and translator. The fascinating discoveries of art and its forms have been a part of her life ever since she was regularly dragged to art exhibitions by her parents as a child.

Now, as an avid enthusiast of galleries and museums around the globe, she jumped at the chance to put together this informative, quirky guide to galleries and installations in the heart of Europe.

Katrin has written two other books. Her most recent—*Flat Switzerland*, about leisurely cycling tours—was published by Helvetiq in 2022.

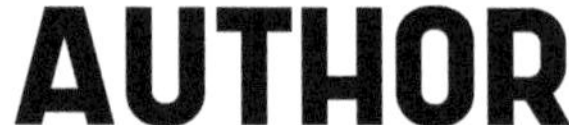

LOCATIONS

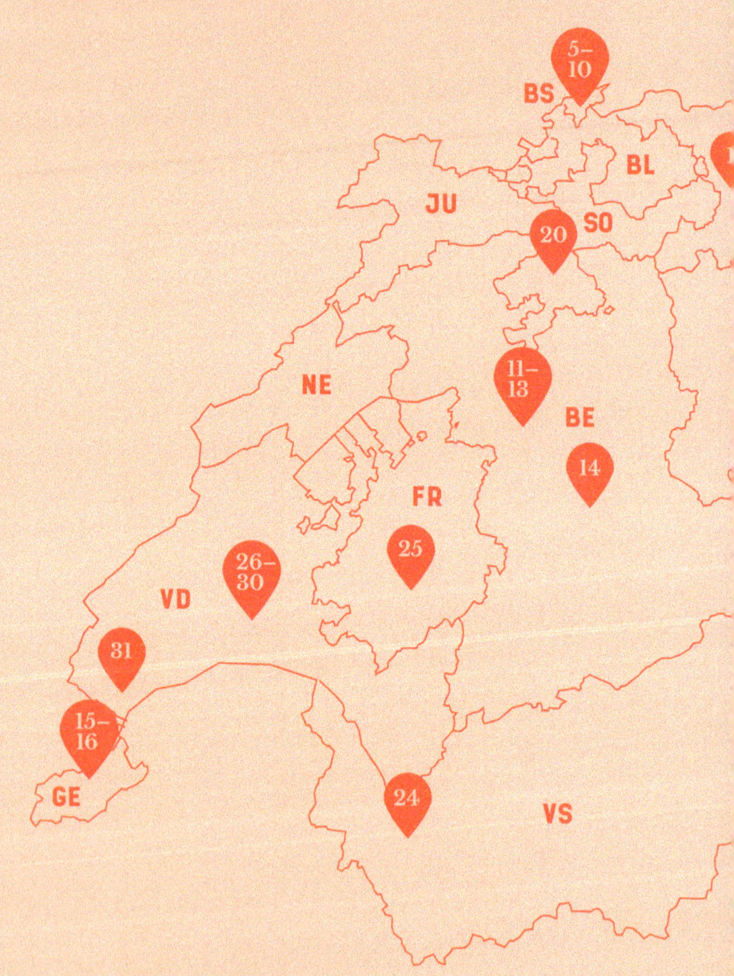

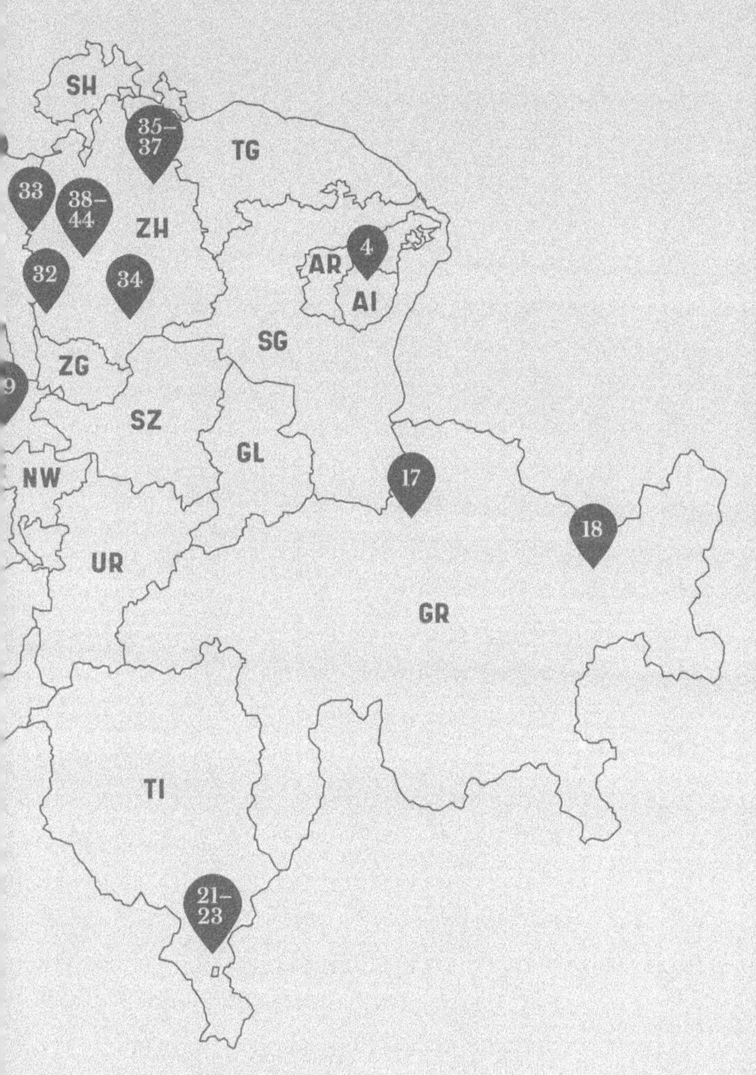

SH
35–
37
TG
33
38–
44
ZH
4
AR
AI
32
34
SG
ZG
SZ
GL
NW
17
18
UR
GR
TI
21–
23